BFI Film Classics

The BFI Film Classics series introduces, interprets and celebrates landmarks of world cinema. Each volume offers an argument for the film's 'classic' status, together with discussion of its production and reception history, its place within a genre or national cinema, an account of its technical and aesthetic importance, and in many cases, the author's personal response to the film.

For a full list of titles in the series, please visit
https://www.bloomsbury.com/uk/series/bfi-film-classics/

Touki Bouki

Rosalind Galt

THE BRITISH FILM INSTITUTE
Bloomsbury Publishing Plc, 50 Bedford Square, London, WC1B 3DP, UK
Bloomsbury Publishing Inc, 1359 Broadway, New York, NY 10018, USA
Bloomsbury Publishing Ireland, 29 Earlsfort Terrace, Dublin 2, D02 AY28, Ireland

BLOOMSBURY is a trademark of Bloomsbury Publishing Plc

First published in Great Britain 2026 by Bloomsbury on behalf of the
British Film Institute, 21 Stephen Street, London, W1T 1LN
www.bfi.org.uk

The BFI is a cultural charity, a National Lottery distributor, and the UK's lead organisation for film and the moving image. We believe society needs stories. Film, television and the moving image bring them to life, helping us to connect and understand each other better. We share the stories of yesterday, search for the stories of today, and shape the stories of tomorrow.

Copyright © Rosalind Galt 2026

Rosalind Galt has asserted her right under the Copyright, Designs and Patents Act, 1988,
to be identified as author of this work.

For legal purposes the Acknowledgments on p. 6 constitute an extension of this copyright page.

Cover artwork: © Ify Chiejina
Series cover design: Louise Dugdale
Series text design: Ketchup/SE14
Images from *Touki Bouki* (Djibril Diop Mambéty, 1973), Cinegrit
Film stills courtesy BFI National Archive
Additional image credits are listed on p. 103

All rights reserved. No part of this publication may be: i) reproduced or transmitted in any form, electronic or mechanical, including photocopying, recording or by means of any information storage or retrieval system without prior permission in writing from the publishers; or ii) used or reproduced in any way for the training, development or operation of artificial intelligence (AI) technologies, including generative AI technologies. The rights holders expressly reserve this publication from the text and data mining exception as per Article 4(3) of the Digital Single Market Directive (EU) 2019/790.

Bloomsbury Publishing Plc does not have any control over, or responsibility for, any third-party websites referred to or in this book. All internet addresses given in this book were correct at the time of going to press. The author and publisher regret any inconvenience caused if addresses have changed or sites have ceased to exist, but can accept no responsibility for any such changes.

A catalogue record for this book is available from the British Library.

Library of Congress Control Number: 2025025915

ISBN: PB: 978-1-8390-2900-4
        ePDF: 978-1-8390-2906-6
        ePUB: 978-1-8390-2902-8

Printed and bound in India

For product safety related questions contact productsafety@bloomsbury.com.

To find out more about our authors and books visit www.bloomsbury.com
and sign up for our newsletters.

Contents

Acknowledgments	6
Introduction	7
1 Africa and Europe	28
2 Liberated Aesthetics	52
3 Embodiment	72
4 Afterlives	89
Notes	95
Credits	104

Acknowledgments

I'm grateful for the help and encouragement of colleagues at King's College London, especially Catherine Wheatley, Lawrence Napper, Nobunye Levin, Tom Brown, Jinhee Choi and Ginette Vincendeau. Karl Schoonover has been talking about African cinemas with me forever and our conversations continue to nourish me intellectually. Some of the research was done at the University of California, Berkeley, where Kristen Whissel, Damon Young and Maya Sidhu offered support both intellectual and brilliantly practical. Huge appreciation goes to Rebecca Barden and Sophie Contento. Last but not least, Adrian Goycoolea and Peter Limbrick are always there for me.

Introduction

In one of *Touki Bouki*'s most striking sequences, a young couple recline in the back of a luxurious convertible car, dressed in ostentatiously high-class European clothes, while snootily enjoying the compliments of a traditional Senegalese praise song. Ne'er-do-well protagonist Mory wears a suit and straw boater and smokes a cigar while his student girlfriend Anta combines a chic lilac jacket, red hat, sunglasses and a retro glamorous cigarette holder. The group singing Mory's praises is led by Aunt Oumy, played by iconic Senegalese singer Aminata Fall, joined by a crowd clapping, cheering and drumming. The scene juxtaposes a colourful visual spectacle of Europeanised wealth with a dynamic display of Senegalese musical heritage, and it playfully subverts ideas about tradition and modernity in postcolonial Africa. *Touki Bouki* is certainly interested in Africa's past and present, but the scene exemplifies its exuberant refusal of representational conventions. Rather than

straightforwardly depicting Senegalese traditions, the praise song is a fantasy sequence that, although Fall's performance displays her authentic off-screen virtuosity, is equally a fiction embedded in the imagination of the film's protagonists. Moreover, Mory and Anta have stolen their chic clothes, and their serving of wealthy European realness is equally fantasmatic. It's not even clear where the fantasy begins and ends, as Anta and Mory's grandiose visions seep into the film's reality. This layering of representation is at the heart of what makes the film so original: against what was seen as the dominant mode of social realism in postcolonial West African cinemas, *Touki Bouki* trades in fantasy, modernism and genre, and takes a queer pleasure in the texture, body and surface of the image.

The many relationships conjured here – between Africa and Europe, tradition and modernity, realism and fantasy, performance and identity, sound and image – are complex, and we can see why *Touki Bouki* has been widely lauded as a classic of African and world cinema. It won the International Critics Award at the Cannes Film Festival in 1973 and the Special Jury Award at the Moscow Film Festival, having an effect in Europe that Catherine Ruelle likened to a slap.[1] In the decades since its release, its reputation has only grown. In 2018, an international jury at the African Film Festival in Tangier named it the best African film in history.[2] Nwachukwu Frank Ukadike calls it 'a tour de force of narrative and technical sophistication', and its formal experimentation led Manthia Diawara to dub it 'the first avant-garde film' from Africa.[3] David Murphy and Patrick Williams describe a consensus that Mambéty was 'the most gifted of all African film directors', and Abou Aziz Sy writes that it is considered to be 'one of the highest achievements in African cinema'.[4] Mambéty's fellow Senegalese film-makers offer their own praise songs: his former assistant director Ben Diogaye Bèye describes his 'total independence of spirit' and 'rare originality', Cheikh Ngaïdo Bâ calls him 'a great humanist' and Moussa Touré terms him simply a visionary.[5]

The film's plot is simple: young couple Mory and Anta are ill at ease in postcolonial Dakar and decide to leave for a new life in Paris. Mory is a former zebu (cattle) herder who is now living in the city and perennially broke. Anta is a free-spirited university student who doesn't fit in either with her family or with the student revolutionaries. Despite more than a decade of independence, they feel trapped by the limited possibilities for social mobility in Senegal. Because they cannot afford to buy a passage to France, they come up with a series of schemes to win, scam or steal the money, moving around the neighbourhoods and subcultures of Dakar as they do so. Eventually, they succeed in stealing enough money for two tickets on the *Ancerville*, a ship departing for Marseille. Both lovers embark but Mory has second thoughts, racing off at the last minute and choosing to remain in Senegal, while Anta sets sail for France. Made in 1973, *Touki Bouki* evokes the energies and frustrations of postcolonial Africa, in which disaffected youth might still have dreamed of the former colonial metropole and yet, unlike many films of emigration, it is wholly invested in creating a Senegalese imaginary. Mambéty's 'slap' of a first feature looks outward to the postcolonial world and evokes global cinematic influences while remaining grounded in the lifeworlds of Dakar and in the liberatory potential of African film aesthetics. *Touki Bouki* is a classic of world cinema, I will argue, because it self-consciously and exhilaratingly reconfigures cinematic worlds.

Touki Bouki's worlds

Let's begin by orienting ourselves to the various 'worlds' that *Touki Bouki* inhabits. Mambéty is often contrasted with other major postcolonial film-makers in West Africa, of whom the most significant is his fellow Senegalese director Ousmane Sembene. Sembene created a mode of politically engaged realist film-making in post-independence Senegal that was hugely influential. Kenneth Harrow writes that Mambéty's vocabulary of marginality and ironic distance, combined with anti-conventional stances and avant-garde filming techniques, shocked African audiences accustomed to the clarity and social commitment of films by Sembene and peers such as Mahama Johnson Traoré, Paulin Vieyra and Ababacar

Samb-Makharam.[6] Whether associated with the postcolonial state, like Vieyra, grounded in ethnology like Safi Faye or combining political critique with African traditions, like Souleymane Cissé, West African cinemas in the years after independence were most often understood as deploying realism in the service of national liberation. Mambéty was just twenty years younger than Sembene, but the idea of socially conscious realism was already well established when his effervescent short films *Contras' City* (1969) and *Badou Boy* (1970) burst onto the scene. For director Mansour Sora Wade, Mambéty responded to things 'as he felt them', in a contrast between a didactic cinema and one of feelings.[7]

Badou Boy (1970) exuberantly follows a young man evading the police in Dakar

These contrasts usefully point to the sheer originality of *Touki Bouki*, its exhilarating aesthetic force. Even viewed for the first time today, its stylistic confidence is breathtaking, sometimes puzzling, always deeply pleasurable. Nonetheless, emphasis on the film's contrast with Sembene and other first-generation West African filmmakers can over-simplify both modes of film-making. Sembene is no straightforward realist and nor is Mambéty apolitical or solely interested in formal experimentation. As David Murphy points out, every member of this generation of postcolonial film-makers was engaged in a rich conversation about the potential for African cinema.[8] For artists who had grown up in a colonial context in which African film-makers were legally proscribed from even using film technology, and who had experienced the struggle for independence, cinema was necessarily socially engaged.

Questions of how to create a national culture, of the relationship between artists and the state, and of what a decolonised aesthetics might look like were the subject of popular debate. Férid Boughedir, the Tunisian director whose 1983 film *Caméra d'Afrique/Twenty Years of African Cinema* documented the first decades of postcolonial film-making, identified a set of common themes, including

the fight against colonialism and neocolonialism, criticism of retrograde traditions ... rejection of the West's alienation ... the rupture between country and city and its consequences, the rural exodus, the demystification of the golden dream of emigrating to Europe, denunciation of the situation of African women.[9]

Many of these themes can be found in *Touki Bouki*, and Mambéty shared with the realist film-makers both a disappointment with postcolonial governments and a belief that African cinema should not be simply entertainment. Cinema mattered and film style also mattered: the imaginative capacities of the medium had previously been used only to create a racist vision of Africa. To counter this colonial legacy, African film-makers were engaged in a wholesale remaking of film form, and the different approaches of Mambéty, Sembene, Faye, Cissé and others reflected the depth and nuance of this creative conversation.

Furthermore, overly rigid contrasts between realism and modernism or politics and style do a disservice to Mambéty's layered film-making, which can be framed in relation to anticolonial Third Cinema, Hollywood genres, European art cinema and to the emerging shapes of world cinema in the 1970s. The film's most obvious intertextual reference is the French New Wave, a connection that has been noted by many critics. Anta and Mory have been described as 'a Senegalese version of Godard's Patricia and Michel in Breathless'.[10] À bout de souffle/Breathless (1960) is also evoked in the film's jazzy soundtrack and editing rhythms, and the use of bold colour is reminiscent of Pierrot le fou (1965). Looking a little further afield, the abattoir sequences evoke Georges Franju's Le Sang des bêtes/Blood of the Beasts (1949). The French newspaper Libération described it as a combination of Pierrot le fou, Bonnie and Clyde (Arthur Penn, 1967) and Cocorico Monsieur Poulet/Cock-a-Doodle-Doo! Mr. Chicken (Jean Rouch, 1974).[11]

Elements of Pierrot le fou (1965) echo in Touki Bouki

Given the French New Wave's investment in reimagining Hollywood B-movies, it is not surprising that *Touki Bouki* is also in conversation with New Hollywood. *Bonnie and Clyde*, with its story of criminal lovers, is a key intertext, but its anti-establishment ethos of youth in revolt also evokes *Easy Rider* (Dennis Hopper, 1969) and *Performance* (Nicolas Roeg, 1970), not to mention Blaxploitation films such as Melvin Van Peebles's *Sweet Sweetback's Baadasssss Song* (1971). Sada Niang suggests an expansive set of counter-cultural references including James Dean on his motorbike and Westerns like *Il buono, il brutto, il cattivo/The Good, the Bad and the Ugly* (Sergio Leone, 1966).[12] That the latter is an Italian Western reminds us of the transnational circulations of film genres in the 1960s and 70s, within which *Touki Bouki* participates in a global network of cinematic influences.

References to Godard, Pasolini, Penn and Leone were common cinematic currency in the 1970s but we can equally trace the importance of radical cinemas for *Touki Bouki*. The film's intellectual montage echoes that of Sergei Eisenstein, not least where *Touki Bouki*, like *Stachka/Strike* (1925), cuts from a kind of violence

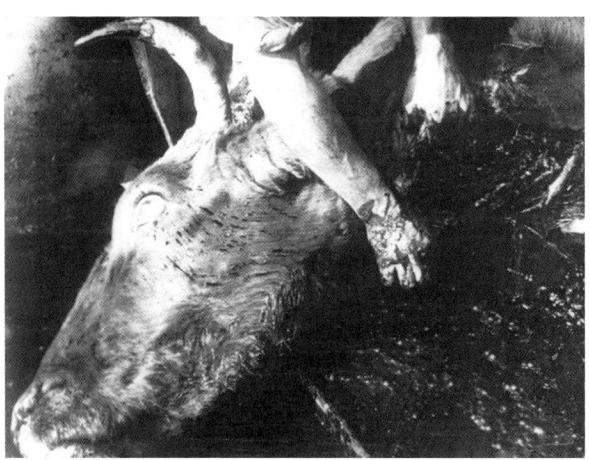

Touki Bouki's zebu evoke the animals of *Strike* (1925)

inflicted on people to scenes of animal slaughter. Contemporary anticolonial cinemas also formed a transnational conversation for African directors: Third Cinema from Argentina and other Latin American, Middle Eastern and Asian film movements offered alternative pathways of inspiration and debate. Mark Cousins suggests that Mambéty's layered sound design draws from the storied Bengali director Ritwik Ghatak, another film-maker who mobilised an original cinematic language to represent the experience of historical trauma.[13] Ukadike compares *Touki Bouki*'s representation of white French neocolonialists to *La hora de los hornos/The Hour of the Furnaces* (Fernando Solanas and Octavio Getino, 1968), an experimental documentary on the history of neocolonialism in Latin America that forms Third Cinema's boldest agitprop experiment.[14] For Jean-Luc Pouillaude, Mambéty's style is even more akin to that of Brazilian Cinema Novo directors Glauber Rocha and Carlos Diegues.[15] Rocha created his own transits of international solidarity, for instance casting French New Wave star Jean-Pierre Léaud in *Der Leone Have Sept Cabeças/The Lion Has Seven Heads* (1970), which was filmed in the Congo. Across this network of references and connections, *Touki Bouki* criss-crosses the imaginative spaces of world cinema.

For an African film, however, this global intertextuality could never be neutral. A western film-maker might draw on the French New Wave merely as a stylistic reference point, but for Mambéty and his peers, their engagement with histories of cinema was always weighed down by colonial mindsets. Kobena Mercer has discussed the way in which European critics can only see formal experimentation in Black cinema as reference to Euro-American avant-garde histories, and this blinkered vision leads to a double bind for a film like *Touki Bouki*.[16] To draw on European cinema is to risk accusations of selling out and making films for westerners, but to abjure these transnational connections would be to buy into a limiting idea of African authenticity and cultural purity. In either case, western critics tended to patronise African films as either derivative or romantically primitive.[17] To reckon with *Touki Bouki*'s place in world cinema is to resist this binary and to see its formal experimentation as both worldly and African.

As western film culture has been increasingly compelled to account for its own colonialist history, it has struggled with how to revise its perspective to account differently for African cinemas. Cousins reflects on this problem when he describes *Touki Bouki* as 'Africa's *Citizen Kane*', going on to reflect on the value of such comparisons. He writes:

To form a canon and have Mambéty talked about in the same way as John Cassavetes, for example, is an entryist strategy. Unless we are happy with the aesthetic, geographical and thematic range of films that are in the air of our film culture (which we most definitely should not be), I believe that we must seek to introduce ignored films – calling them lost classics if necessary – into the canon ... How many of these who revered 8½ (Federico Fellini, 1963) or *Rashomon* (Akira Kurosawa, 1950) had ever heard of *Touki Bouki*?[18]

This kind of comparison uses well-known reference points like *Citizen Kane* (Orson Welles, 1941) to expand the canon, but of course (and Cousins is aware of this problem) it also maintains Hollywood and the West as the basis for understanding cinematic quality. How can we add *Touki Bouki* to a pre-existing canon of classics, allowing it to speak alongside these great films, while also disrupting the force of a critical hierarchy that was built and has been maintained by a colonialist worldview? African cinemas were not accidentally omitted from the canon but systematically excluded.

Rather than asking the world cinema canon to accommodate *Touki Bouki*, we need to account for why it was not recognised before. The fact that it was indigestible, made invisible or overlooked is part of the story. Kenyan writer Ngũgĩ wa Thiong'o's *Moving the Centre* offers an influential model for shifting our assumptions about where the global centres of culture are located and where we should direct our attention.[19] Ella Shohat and Robert Stam similarly propose a 'polycentric aesthetics' of world cinema to overcome histories of European and Hollywood-centrism.[20] A polycentric approach pays attention to regional differences. For instance, Achille Mbembe and Sarah Nuttall argue that modern worldliness in Africa

> has had to do not only with the capacity to generate one's own cultural forms, institutions, and lifeways, but also the ability to foreground, translate, fragment, and disrupt realities and imaginaries originating elsewhere, and in the process place these forms and processes in the service of one's own making.[21]

These and other postcolonial thinkers have proposed new ways to visualise the shapes of world cinema, and throughout this analysis, worldliness will be a recurring framework: what does it mean to think about *Touki Bouki* as a classic of world cinema, how can we understand movements and styles as speaking across cultures, and how does *Touki Bouki* itself imagine the world that it represents, and the audiences that it addresses?

These might seem like large-scale or even abstract issues, but in order to think about what makes *Touki Bouki* a classic, they are unavoidable. Every critic of the film has had an opinion about what it means for Mambéty to draw from transnational sources. If western cinema formed the horizon of knowledge for European critics, leading them to misunderstand African films, African critics sometimes championed films that more directly rejected western aesthetics. *Touki Bouki* prompted lively debate in the Senegalese press, with Dakar's main daily newspaper asking whether the film was made for 'educated Dakar youth, global African youth, or Western film buffs'.[22] The film's relationships to African culture, to European art cinema and to anticolonial cinemas place it at the heart of debates on decolonising the mind, on cultures of liberation and on the futures of African cinemas. One of the great pleasures of *Touki Bouki* is that is enables the viewer to experience these questions not as a heavy contextual burden but as a brilliant and exuberant cinematic experience.

Mambéty himself writes that

> I am interested in marginalized people, because I believe that they do more for the evolution of a community than the conformists. Marginalized people bring a community into contact with a wider world. The characters of *Touki-Bouki* are interesting to me because their dreams are not those of ordinary people. Anta and Mory do not dream of building castles in Africa; they dream of finding some sort of Atlantis overseas.[23]

Marginalised people for him create contact zones, characters who can make friction between spaces and cultures. Whereas Mambéty himself was deeply committed to building a film culture in Africa, his characters are neither idealists nor ideologues – they dream of elsewheres. Mambéty's son, Teemour Diop Mambéty, described his father as uninhibited in both creation and life, working to mould an African identity while still being universal, both discovering the world and being discovered by it. To be uninhibited, he says, is to be open to the world.[24] *Touki Bouki* is intimately embedded in the local life of Dakar, and it is from there that it looks out to the world. For Mambéty, contact between Senegal and a wider world is not a dream of cinephile universalism but a vision of global film style meeting the needs of Africans.

Biography

Djibril Diop Mambéty was born in 1945 in Colobane, a Dakar neighbourhood that would feature in many of his films. He was the son of an imam and was educated by his grandmother, Mame Betty, from whom he took his name.[25] (The wisdom of grandmothers was to be important to his film-making: the grandmother embodies a passing down of knowledge but also resistance to stifling institutions.) Although his parents knew nothing about film, Djibril and his brother, Wasis, liked to listen outside the local cinema.

Djibril Diop Mambéty photographed in 1992

'I wanted to make films,' Mambéty often recalled in interviews, 'so in the yard at home, with a white sheet, a candle behind it and cut-out images, friends in front, we made our own cinema, adding the images from our imagination to the sounds we listened to.'[26] Wasis Diop describes him as a precocious child, who skipped school to take his brother on adventures around Dakar. He credits becoming a jazz musician to these early experiences of listening to the culture around them. As a child, Djibril told his father that he just wanted to understand the world.[27]

Mambéty studied drama and become an actor at the Daniel Sorano National Theatre in Dakar. He was dismissed for indiscipline, however, and this challenge prompted him to pursue cinema on his own. At the age of only twenty-one, he borrowed a camera from the French Cultural Centre and made an early version of *Badou Boy*, a kinetic short film about a young man on the run from a policeman.[28] The film screened at the inaugural Festival mondial des arts nègres in 1966, a prestigious gathering of Black talent from around the world including luminaries like James Baldwin, Aimé Césaire, Duke Ellington and Katherine Dunham, as well as a prominent role for Ousmane Sembene. Mambéty was inspired by this celebration of Black cultures and by the passionate debates around African art and politics. This was a period of extraordinary artistic flourishing in Dakar, and Mambéty was part of a vibrant cultural scene. His friends included the singer Aminata Fall, musician Billy Kongoma, sculptor Joe Ouakam and film-maker Ben Diogaye Bèye.[29] Friends described him as charismatic, generous and handsome, a dandy who always made an impression. He did not only move in artistic circles, though. He was equally at home in upscale or lower-class environments; in the words of Laurence Gavron, he could open any door.[30]

Unlike many African film-makers of the early generation, Mambéty was not formed by travelling overseas. Unlike Sembene, he did not study film-making in Moscow, and, unlike Med Hondo, he did not spend his formative years working in France. He was self-taught as a film-maker, learning from his peers in the Dakar arts community and from his role as the secretary of the Dakar ciné-club.[31] Xavier Villetard describes him as the only African to have made a film without having set foot in Europe, and this background helps account for his unique style.[32] Moreover, many Senegalese film-makers cut their teeth making newsreels, a state-sponsored route into film-making that provided limited formal training and which Mambéty also eschewed.[33] He did visit Europe, though. After making *Badou Boy*, Mambéty spent a few months in Marseille, travelling on the same ship that features in *Touki Bouki*. This experience 'shattered his long-held illusions about the mythical world of the former colonial power', a response that would certainly have echoed that of Paulin Vieyra, Sembene and other West African film-makers of the period.[34] Upon his return, he began work on *Touki Bouki*.

The making of *Touki Bouki*

In making *Touki Bouki*, Mambéty drew on his creative friendships. Sada Niang suggests that he brought from theatre a desire to work with a group and an idea of exchange as foundational to artistic creation.[35] Thus, his friend Ben Diogaye Bèye served as his assistant director and the DP was Georges Bracher, a French cinematographer who had settled in Dakar and collaborated with many Senegalese film-makers. He cast singer Aminata Fall as Aunt Oumy, alongside Magaye Niang as Mory and Myriam Niang as Anta. The latter became a significant presence in the Dakar film-making scene, playing roles in Momar Thiam's *Baks* (1974), which was co-written by Bèye, as well as in Sembene's *Xala* (1975), both of which ended up on Dakarois screens at the same time as *Touki Bouki*. With these collaborators, Mambéty encouraged improvisation. Bèye recalls spending every night before the shoot with a group of friends in restaurants and bars, talking about the film. Whenever anyone

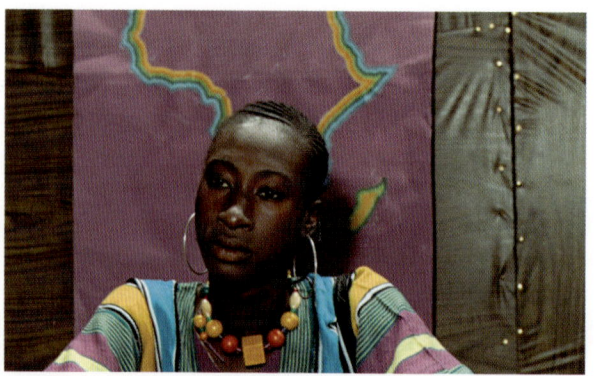

Myriam Niang is a prominent actor in *Xala* (1975)

suggested something amusing that could be added to the script, Djibril would say 'yes, why not do that!'[36] Moreover, he didn't accept ideas only from his friends: that childhood idea of learning from the streets of Dakar continued as a way of life. Quotidian encounters with acquaintances and strangers, often in the less salubrious bars of the city, made their way into the world of the film. Despite this creative openness, *Touki Bouki* is carefully constructed. Bèye describes Mambéty preparing shots and colour choices scrupulously, and Cheikh Ngaïdo Bâ says that 'Everything he did was calculated.'[37] This mixture of careful formal layering and exhilarating openness to the world characterises the film's liberatory energy.

Touki Bouki's production was enabled by a short-lived period in which Senegalese film-making was supported by both the Senegalese state and, albeit in a problematic way, by the French Ministry of Cooperation. Léopold Sédar Senghor's government instituted the Société National du Cinéma in 1973 and *Touki Bouki* was among the first films to receive a subvention. Mambéty augmented this state funding with prize money garnered in Italy by *Badou Boy*.[38] These sources of income allowed Mambéty to be relatively independent and in particular free of the restrictions faced by film-makers reliant on French funding. The French Ministry of Cooperation was created in 1963 to provide technical and financial assistance to France's former colonies and this office had funded almost 200 films by 1975.[39] As Claire Andrade-Watkins argues, however, the primary aim of this funding mechanism was to perpetuate a colonialist logic of assimilation to French culture, making it 'the means by which postcolonial cultural dominance was maintained'.[40] The Ministry tied the films it funded into non-theatrical distribution deals, which made it very difficult to release them commercially. *Touki Bouki*, like most Senegalese films, was stuck with this deal, whereby rights were ceded for five years in return for 30,000 francs towards costs such as editing, lab work and prints.[41]

Many of Mambéty's peers were compelled by the terms of their contracts to edit their films in Paris, working with French editors for whom the assignment was a low-prestige gig to be handled as rapidly as possible. These editors did not understand the priorities of the African directors they were working with and those directors, in turn, often did not have the technical training to pull rank. Thus, the editing of African films made in this way was often boringly conventional. Mambéty's stronger financial position enabled him to avoid this fate by working on editing and sound mixing in Rome.[42] *Touki Bouki*'s montage is exuberant and utterly distinctive, as is the film's experimental discontinuity of sound and image, so Djibril's ability to manage postproduction independently was a crucial factor in the film's final shape. His time in Rome was not entirely smooth, though. On 25 April 1973, Mambéty participated in an anti-racist demonstration and was arrested and charged with assaulting a police officer. He spent five weeks in prison and was released only after Italian friends including Bernardo Bertolucci and Sophia Loren arranged for a lawyer from the Italian Communist Party (PCI) to bail him out. To add further insult, when he returned to Senegal, Mambéty received a bill from the PCI for their legal services![43] The experience may have left an imprint on the final film. Mambéty has said that if it had not been for his incarceration, he would not have used such bloody abattoir images.[44]

Exhibition and reception

Touki Bouki opened in Senegal on 29 March 1975 and played at nineteen cinemas around Dakar until 22 May. Its release was accompanied by much fanfare: one large advertisement in the daily newspaper *Le Soleil* proclaimed, 'Here finally in Dakar! … The new triumph of Senegalese cinema', and another declared, 'Bravo la SIDEC!', heralding the role of Senghor's government in funding the nascent local film industry.[45] (*Le Soleil* was associated with Senghor.) The film premiered at the upscale Plaza cinema in the central Plateau neighbourhood and then moved to the Vog and the ABC, where it was advertised as 'An immense success! A film that you absolutely must see!'[46] In the following weeks, the Al Akhbar

An advertisement for *Touki Bouki*'s release in Senegalese newspaper *Le Soleil* (1975) (courtesy British Library)

cinema proclaimed, 'Paris is finished!', and the Magic promised 'a great film by Djibril Diop Mambéty'.[47] From the chichi cinemas in the Plateau, *Touki Bouki* moved out to cinemas in more working-class neighbourhoods like the Medina, Colobane and Pikine. The Star cinema advertised it as 'another Senegalese success', the immediate point of comparison being Sembene's *Xala*, which had opened the week before and which was an even higher-profile product of the national cinema.[48]

The standard narrative about *Touki Bouki* is that it flopped in Senegal. For Bèye, 'the film didn't work at all here' and various writers have claimed that it screened for only four days.[49] That is not true, as its run of almost two months indicates. It sometimes played at a particular cinema for only a few days, but that was fairly typical of the way films circulated in the Dakar cinemas. Various critics have repeated the claim that the film was barely seen in Senegal, which does not match with its exhibition all across Dakar and the many column inches devoted to it in the Senegalese press. Why the confusion? The misremembered account has perhaps acquired 'print the legend' status because it creates a metaphor of what did happen, which is that *Touki Bouki* provoked a controversy about what Senegalese cinema should be.

For the film's detractors, it was both too experimental and overly negative about Senegalese society. Latyr Mbassou Diouf calls films like *Touki Bouki*, *Baks* and *Xala* 'turnips' and says they are too miserable, showing juvenile delinquents, crime and an overall negative vision of the country.[50] (This complaint is similar to those who feared that the films of Roberto Rossellini and Satyajit Ray were washing their respective nations' dirty laundry in public.) *Touki Bouki*'s marginal protagonists were also a problem for critics who disapproved of its focus on 'a delinquent', a 'rich homosexual' and 'a girl who we wondered if she was not a boy'.[51] These writers articulate a culturally conservative perspective. They want a more conventional national cinema, both in terms of class and gender representation and film form. M. Dia wonders how *Touki Bouki* could possibly have won prizes and A. P. Diop describes the audience at the screening he attended as doubting the competence of the director. They excoriate *Touki Bouki* as mediocre, incomprehensible and poorly made.[52]

Such negative response clearly hit Mambéty hard and yet many writers took to the pages of *Le Soleil* to defend him. Kemal Ndiaye is 'very disappointed' that the public did not appreciate *Touki Bouki*, which he says is 'one of the most beautiful' Senegalese films. Pierre Souillac calls Mambéty 'a great poet of the screen' and the newspaper's main film reviewer, Le Cyclope, dubs it 'a landmark in the history of African cinema'.[53] Several reviewers emphasised the film's artistic qualities, comparing it to reading a novel by Proust and suggesting that the audience who couldn't understand the film are just like those French audiences who couldn't understand Miró and Ernst. Responding to those who would compare *Touki Bouki*'s experimental form negatively with Sembene's realism, Souillac argues that Senegalese cinema needs both its Rimbaud and its Molière.[54] Anne Marty bemoans the lack of arts education that prevented the public from being able to understand it, and Wolfgang von Wangenheim deems Mambéty 'a visionary poet whom we will understand one day'.[55]

In addition to championing *Touki Bouki*'s aesthetic radicalism, the film's supporters saw in it a valuable political contribution to young Senegalese cinema. Le Cyclope argues that *Touki Bouki* opens up both a Black collective unconscious and a willingness to violate the taboos of the modern era. 'So what colour is the opponent?', they ask. 'Alas for all those who think that world history is a black and white film, the enemy of the ex-colonised … is not necessarily white.'[56] Pape Samba Ba finds Diouf's criticism to be 'destructive and unjustified' and, along with several other critics, insists that films like *Touki Bouki* and *Baks* must engage with real social problems in order to encourage reflection and healing.[57] The writers defending *Touki Bouki* are aligned with a more progressive group who encouraged the imagination and aesthetic ambition of Senegalese cinema. Cheikh Kane, for instance, insists that a national cinema should not merely reflect local realities, and Moustafa Diouf argues that it's wrong to call Senegalese cinema miserable and that, after those in the Maghreb, Senegal's film-makers are the best in Africa.[58] Spanning address, popular audiences, film style and engagement with social problems, the *Touki Bouki* debate exemplifies in a nutshell the major issues facing African cinemas in the postcolonial world.

Touki Bouki's detractors were the more powerful faction, however, and Mambéty found himself out of favour with the

Senegalese film establishment. Along with his friend Joe Ouakam, he had founded the Laboratoire Agit'Art, a radical art collective, but was unable to secure funding to make another feature film until *Hyènes/Hyenas* in 1992. The same conservative forces thwarted *Touki Bouki*'s international profile. After its triumph at Cannes, it was not seen in Europe for over a decade and James Williams asserts that 'it was deliberately "lost" by powerful institutional forces within African cinema'.[59] In the 1980s, it was rediscovered

Mambéty's late film *Le Franc* (1994)

by cineastes: screenings at the Museum of Modern Art in New York and in a 'Racines noires' series in Paris prefigured a theatrical release in France in 1986. Seen as something of a *film maudit*, its belated cinematic release prompted reassessment. *Le Monde* acclaimed it as a 'film-surprise', while *Libération* asked how a film that is legendary across Africa could have remained unseen for so long. 'Is it because it was too beautiful?'[60] *Variety* described Mambéty as a newcomer who 'makes an impact', and a screening in Ouagadougou made a very concrete impact, raising 130,000 CFA francs, which Mambéty donated to a maternity hospital in the city.[61]

Touki Bouki's refusal to fit neatly into either nationalist realism or political modernism meant that Mambéty was not well understood in the context of 1970s film cultures, but his rediscovery prompted a late burst of creativity, including *Hyenas*, as well as *Parlons grand-mère* (1989), *Le Franc* (1994) and *La Petite Vendeuse de soleil/ The Little Girl Who Sold the Sun* (1999), the latter of which was released posthumously after he died of lung cancer at the age of only fifty-three. Since Mambéty's death, his films have been increasingly recognised. On the tenth anniversary of his death, memorial events were held in Senegal, France and Tunisia.[62] Mambéty's son has worked on restoring his father's films to make them available for new generations.[63] In 2013, *Touki Bouki* was restored by Martin Scorsese's World Cinema Project, as a result of which it has found a new worldwide audience. As Mambéty himself said about the future of African film-making, 'It is almost too late, but it is never too late for beauty.'[64]

1 Africa and Europe

Touki Bouki takes the form of a journey. Its title translates as 'the hyena's journey' and its narrative leads us from the landscape of the Sahel through the neighbourhoods of Dakar to the harbour, where Anta leaves Africa for Europe and Mory chooses to stay. This trajectory forms a self-conscious reflection on the film's own place in the world: it asks what it means to be an African film in the circulatory spaces of world cinema, just as Anta and Mory must consider where and how they want to be in the world. Djibril Diop Mambéty describes *Touki Bouki* as

> about those days when we dreamed of going abroad. We dreamed the white's dream of making movies. It was as if we were foreigners in our own homes here in Africa. Foreigners because our 'everything' was abroad. It is there that you go to succeed, to make pictures. Then when you come back, people will call you 'sir.' Then we say, 'Well, we need to travel.' 'But how will you go?' 'Oh, there are ships here!' 'But how much does it cost?' 'Oh, there are ways!' 'But why are you going there?' 'When we get there with our beauty, with our stature, with our blackness, people will clap their hands, and say, "Here is the king, the ruler."' This was our dream, and in dreaming this, we forgot our own country. What a pity! Twenty-five years later, I realized that it was not true. I escaped from that ugly dream. I wanted my generation and all Africans to escape from that dream too. And build our country where we are not foreigners. Forget those dreams of elsewhere. Let us dream our dreams and plant our seeds here in Africa. That is what I felt when I made *Touki Bouki*.[65]

This chapter explores what the dream of emigration means to *Touki Bouki*'s young protagonists and how it is transformed in the spaces of postcolonial Senegal. In Senegal or France, at home or as immigrants, Mory and Anta must reckon with the afterlife of European colonialism and yet they are never fully contained by it. Malian filmmaker Souleymane Cissé describes *Touki Bouki* as prophetic of the twenty-first century's experience of young Africans desperately trying to reach Europe by boat.[66] For contemporary audiences, the film surely does speak to this crisis and yet it also articulates a very different cinematic relationship between Africa and Europe.

Touki Bouki has been described as a 'road movie that doesn't go anywhere'.[67] This neat formulation speaks to the way the film begins and ends in the same place, but it also draws attention to where the film does go, which is Dakar. The Senegalese capital was a significant hub for both West African cinemas and postcolonial modernity more broadly. It had been the site of government for the colonial Afrique Occidentale Française (AOF) and it was still, in the 1970s, a regional centre. The postcolonial government, under Léopold Sédar Senghor, had transformed the cityscape with ambitious infrastructural projects as well as hosting cultural events like the international Black arts festival. The city was nonetheless still marked by the hierarchies of the colonial era, separated into the European architecture of the central Plateau and the poverty of the surrounding shanty towns. Matthew Mananga describes it as an example of the periurban condition, in which agriculture, industry and housing all mix in a hybrid space.[68] In this dynamic topos, we also find the creativity of Achille Mbembe's distinctive African modernity.[69] In the decade after independence, Dakar became what James Williams describes as 'the seed-bed for a golden age of prodigious innovation and experimentation – a shining beacon of radical Third Cinema inspiring some of the greatest African films by Sembene, Mambéty, and many others'.[70] For these Senegalese film-makers, reimagining Dakar outside of the colonial worldview was an urgent project of decolonising the mind. *Touki Bouki* is not merely set in Dakar; it creates a radical vision from the myriad experiences of urban life.[71] From the abattoir to the beach villa, the wrestling arena to the dock, Mory and Anta's interior journey takes place in Dakar's real spaces. To unfold *Touki Bouki*'s journey, we will trace (some of) the film's route through the city.

From the Sahel to the sea

We begin outside the city, in a bucolic scene of a boy herding zebu in the dusty landscape of the Sahel. The camera is static, Fulani flute music plays and the cattle walk sedately towards the camera. Any expectations we might have of a gentle rural story are quickly shattered by a cut to the interior of a slaughterhouse. A close-up of a zebu's face

is succeeded by the terrified beast being tied down and its throat slit, with sounds of human shouting and bovine mooing accompanying shots of blood on the floor and walls. The Seras abattoir, to the northeast of the city, was built by the French and remained a central site for animal processing in the postcolonial era. In *Touki Bouki*'s opening, it functions as a space of transformation: from livestock to meat, from rural to urban, from cinematic realism to modernist montage, and from precolonial tradition to the shock of a violent modernity.

Back outside the abattoir, the boy on the zebu is overlaid with the disjunctive sound of a motorbike and we cut to Mory, riding a bike with zebu horns on the handlebars through the streets of the working-class neighbourhood of Colobane. The transition from child to man via the same soundtrack of flute and motorbike implies that Mory is the little zebu herder grown up, and in this new environment the cinematic language also shifts. Instead of a static scene with figures moving from background to foreground, here the camera moves with the bike and lateral point-of-view shots reveal a dynamic social space of people and buildings along the street and into a square. Children run alongside Mory's bike shouting as he heads onto the main highway into the city centre. This is highway N1 through

Colobane, almost at the end point of a road that traverses the entire country. When we cut away from the bike to a wider reverse shot, we see him approach one of the pedestrian bridges that lead towards the Medina and city centre, a piece of urban infrastructure whose metaphoric potential to capture the distance between Black and white Dakar was already familiar from Sembene's *La Noire de …/Black*

Girl (1966) and Mambéty's own *Badou Boy*. One of the bridges features a tourist advert for Nice, the French Riviera and Corsica, a poster addressed to the wealthy who drive along the highway rather than the local population who live beside it. As Mory speeds away, we can see in the distance the white high-rises of the wealthy Plateau.

Touki Bouki calls back to the iconic bridge in *Black Girl* (1966)

We cut away from Mory to a postman trudging slowly across the bridge, carrying letters from relatives who have left for France. From the stairs, we pan across the roofs of Colobane's informal architecture. Another panning shot contrasts the impoverished wooden dwellings of the neighbourhood with the modern city-centre skyline, including the minaret of the Grand Mosque. At ground level, we are introduced to Anta, sitting at an outdoor wooden desk, trying to write while surrounded by urban noise: an aeroplane, the chanting of an imam, a baby crying, a dog barking and a siren squealing. We cut among the postman moving through the streets, Anta's mother selling vegetables at a stall and Anta, trying to focus on her university work. The sonic intrusions come to a head as we hear Anta, off screen, exclaim 'merde!', leading these figures to intersect. Anta's mother complains to a customer that the postman has no letter from her son in France. The customer replies that nothing good ever comes from France and that men who leave bring back white women and their diseases. She wants to take tomatoes on credit but Anta bursts onto the scene and grabs the basket, insisting that she pay immediately. The whole interaction takes place with a static camera until Anta arrives and prompts a match on action cut

as she grabs for the basket. As with Mory, she introduces a mobility and responsiveness in the camera, a shift from static narration to a modern cutting into space. She disrupts the carefully scripted politeness of the encounter as well as troubling social norms and ways of being. Her mother berates her for dating Mory and for being a university student: to her, the university, like France, is an overly modern 'freak show'. The scene ends with Anta running off as her mother shouts after her.

Anta and Mory are rebels but they're not revolutionaries. Emmanuelle Chérel points out that they embody a youth that desires freedom from a colonial mentality they associate with both familial and political authority. They aren't engaged in either the revisionist traditions advocated by nationalist politicians or the Marxism of student radicals.[72] Thus, when Anta gets to the university, she's not interested in the well-dressed students who harass her from their jeep, calling her sexually impure and demanding to know when she'll join their revolution. Worse, these same students kidnap Mory and tie him to their vehicle with rope. (There is a subversive dig at middle-class Marxism here.) The university is verdant with grass as well-tended as the students' chic

Burberry-style plaid outfits, but this moneyed haven of activism at the heart of the city is not a safe space for either of the lovers. Instead, they reunite at Cap Manuel, a wild cliff at the southern tip of Dakar's promontory.

After a sexual encounter that we will discuss in Chapter 2, the couple lie naked on a concrete platform looking out to the Atlantic Ocean. It is here that they first propose leaving Senegal for France. Over a shot of a tiny sailing boat on the sparkling sea, we hear Mory's voice-off saying, 'There's a boat leaving tomorrow, let's take it.' He is referring to an ocean liner and the slippage is what André Gardies calls a 'flottement sémantique', a hesitation of meaning that can also imply floating.[73] We float between the small boat that they see and the large ship that Mory evokes in the future. The couple are framed between land and sea, on the edge of an imagined world beyond Dakar. Anta asks if he has the money for the passage and Mory replies that they don't need money; they will dress up, pretend to be rich and go illegally. Paris is the gateway to paradise, he says (a trope to which we will return), and when they come back to Senegal, they'll be big shots. As Malini Guha argues, the fantasy of migration and return 'allows the journey

itself to operate as a profound indictment of the unequal relations of political and economic power between African nations like Senegal and the former imperial nations including France'.[74] Mobility in the postcolonial world implies a disjuncture and a refusal of the status quo.

Later, Anta and Mory will visit another beach, further up the coast in Ngor by the Almadies lighthouse. This beach is located at the westernmost point of Africa, the very edge of the continent as it extends out towards the world beyond the Atlantic. They look at a shipwreck and dream of repairing the wreck and sailing to Europe. Mambéty has noted that all his stories lead to the sea and that on the Dakar coast, he feels as if he's at the centre of the world.[75] For Giuseppe Gariazzo, the sea in *Touki Bouki* becomes a border to be confronted, and in these scenes, both impulses meet like shore and sea. The westernmost point of Africa is at once central to an imagined Atlantic world and at the edge of the protagonists' horizon of knowledge. The coast both opens to elsewheres and forms a limit, beyond which one needs significant resources to travel. It is on this beach that Mory comes up with the plan that will finally enable them to buy tickets to France.

Cultural spaces

Anta and Mory are alienated from Senegalese society: Sada Niang points out that they only dream of consuming, never of producing, and all their plans for the future involve stealing or otherwise scamming their way to wealth.[76] A social critique runs through the film, in which these marginal lovers embody a disillusionment with post-independence nationalism that Kate Bonin describes as shared by 'a new generation of Africans [who] did not readily identify either with Negritude's promise of timeless pan-African inclusivity – nor did they necessarily feel at home in a Senegal still presided over by Senghor (who would not leave office until 1980)'.[77] The ongoing power of colonial elites, poverty, corruption, police repression and the lack of robust democracy led to widespread discontent. Those critics who disliked the film were perhaps uncomfortable with its animation of the antisocial consequences of this malaise, including Anta and Mory's disaffected scheming. Their enrichment plans take them to various sites of public and private leisure activity in Dakar, spaces of culture in which money might accumulate.

Their first plan is to win the money in a card game in Colobane market. As the couple look down onto the bustling market from a bridge, we hear the voice of a card sharp running a game. Mory has stolen a good luck charm, and this leads him to insist on a large bet when it is his turn to gamble. When he loses, he runs away rather than pay up and the dealer shouts for the crowd to chase him. There follows a long high-angle shot of a crowd in pursuit, then Mory makes his escape down an alley. He stops, slips and regains his balance in a moment that gestures towards his slipping and sliding around legality and urban space.

The next plan is Anta's: she notes that wrestling arenas take a lot of money on Sundays, and we cut to *djembe* drums and then stands full of people at the Iba Mar Diop stadium in the Medina. Wrestling, or *lamb*, is a hugely popular sport in Senegal and this footage from a real match places Anta and Mory in the very centre of popular culture. Paulin Vieyra's documentary *Lamb* (1964)

describes it as 'a true national sport', but it was also promoted by Senghor's government and was thus associated with an official vision of national identity (Vieyra's film has been seen as propagandist).[78] According to the match announcer, this bout is raising money for a Charles de Gaulle memorial, thus humorously emphasising the proximity of sport and neocolonialism. A couple stand up and make their way through the crowd and we realise that they are Anta and Mory, disguised in traditional clothes. She wears a long burgundy patterned *boubou* with matching headwrap and long earrings, while he sports a long metallic kaftan with a scarf tied Berber-style over his face. That they don this traditional drag for the purposes of theft is a sign of their rejection of the official version of national culture.

Outside the stadium, they watch a cop guarding two trunks and debate which one might be full of money. We never see the theft itself but cut directly to a shot of the blue trunk atop a taxi, and then back and forth from the trunk to Mory on his motorbike reflecting on his plans for the money. They proceed through the European part of Dakar, the Plateau, and we even see the Paris cinema in front of Mory, right next to the Délégation Générale

au Tourisme. As Josephine Baker sings 'Paris, Paris, Paris' on the soundtrack, Mory's voiceover imagines that in Paris, he will hit on all the girls and move in all the right circiles. They drive with the trunk past the Chamber of Commerce, the Ministry of Foreign Affairs and through the central Place de l'Indépendance, mocking these national institutions with their outlaw procession. The scheme backfires, however, when they reach what Anta refers to as her summer house, a dilapidated concrete ruin on the cape, looking out past the city to remote Sarpent Island. The taxi driver is creeped out and says, 'You must not be Wolof. Only white people could live out here.' He runs away altogether when he opens the trunk to discover it contains a skull and other charms, but no money.

Their final, successful, plan is to steal from Charlie, a rich gay man of Mory's acquaintance. From the public spaces of market and wrestling arena, they travel to Charlie's upscale modern beach villa, where we encounter him in a pedalo in his swimming pool, surrounded by friends and hangers-on. This queer social scene introduces us to subcultural Dakar, a space that is hiding in plain sight and which provides a contact zone for rich and poor, gay and straight. I'll discuss Charlie more in Chapter 3 but for now we can note his warning to Mory that 'France isn't what it used to be'. He reels off neighbourhoods – 'Champs-Élysées, Pigalle, Montparnasse' – and offers a real-life version of Mory's dream that one could voyage to Paris and return with wealth and status. Mory is quite willing to achieve Charlie's success by stealing from him, however, and the couple flee the fancy villa in Charlie's own car, loaded with stolen money and clothes.

Fantasy Dakar/fantasy Paris

With their ill-gotten gains, Mory and Anta enter a fantasy space in which they have already been to France and returned as celebrities. The couple con Charlie's chauffeur into driving them to the Plateau; en route, reality starts to unravel. Standing shockingly naked in the back of Charlie's convertible, fist in the air, Mory talks himself up like a wrestler, declaiming his victories. Looking out from the car, we see children implausibly run alongside, as they did in Colobane at the beginning of the film, but a reverse angle reveals the car still in the hinterlands and nobody alongside. Disparate times and spaces are sutured together as our image of city begins to reflect Mory and Anta's projection.

Driving into the central streets of the Plateau, they imagine a cavalcade of cheering crowds has been laid on for them. Mory and Anta sit in the back of the car, waving like royalty to their adoring subjects as they pass landmarks like the IBM building. Low-angle shots look up at the couple, using cinematic form ironically to present them as if they were VIPs. Supposed reverse shots depict crowds lining the streets, cheering and drumming, waving national flags. A brass band plays and a procession of soldiers on horses precedes a cavalcade of official black cars. These shots are documentary footage of Gabonese President Omar Bongo's state visit to Senegal in 1974, repurposed as Mory's self-aggrandising fantasy. In a travelling shot past the presidential palace, soldiers in dress uniform line up outside. Although they are in more or less the same places, it is visibly clear that this is newsreel footage. The suturing of shots and locations is disjunctive, because this Dakar of Bongo and Senghor, of palaces and crowds, does not really belong to Mory and Anta.

After the praise song from Aunt Oumy that I discussed in the introduction, the couple return to the Plateau. They cross the road in front of the Comptoir Franco-Suisse at the bottom of the Place de l'Indépendance and walk through a modern arcade towards a

travel agency. We are no longer in Mory's fantasy, yet here in the real commercial centre of Dakar, the couple are still wearing their stolen European outfits. The travel agent is also a site of imagined Europes, with posters for Pam Am and Alitalia airlines. These fantasies can be real, for the wealthy. From the unattainable ad for the French Riviera on the Colobane bridge, we have travelled to the part of the city in which such tourism is within reach. Anta acquires a nouveau riche persona as she purchases tickets to France. The agent asks if she has seen her somewhere before and Anta replies, in French, that it must surely have been in New York. She adopts French as a class marker along with her clothes, using language as a form of neocolonial drag.[79] In this Dakar, at least as Anta imagines it, international travel is a commonplace. Anna Livia sees Mambéty as

using the conventions of European cinema against it. He sets the audience up by citing well-known scenes, like the triumphal parade, the young couple gone bad, or the longed-for trip to Paris, and then challenges our expectations by parodying their Eurocentric underpinnings.[80]

In their stolen attire, Anta and Mory transform both their appearances and their ability to move through Dakar and the world. The final stage of their route takes them to Dakar's port, where the ship to Marseille awaits.

The port and the *Ancerville*

Our first sight of the entrance to the Port of Dakar is a sign that reads 'no entry without authorisation'. A young man stands guard in front of it, menacingly holding a wooden bat. Indeed, before Anta and Mory reach the security gate, a vignette plays out with an unknown character trying to gain access to the port. In voiceover, this man complains, 'This city's rough. No entry on the right, no entry on the left, men with clubs everywhere. All because there are too many debts.' Anta recognises the man as a scam artist named Margot and she and Mory help him get past the guard in their (stolen) car.

The port is the gateway to Europe and this scene humorously stages how economic inequality limits access to Dakar's global infrastructures. Once past security, we follow the car towards the dock and down a quay under imposing, bright yellow cast-iron structures to a ship. The ship is the French liner the *Ancerville*. It was built in 1962 and for the following decade it routed between Dakar

and Marseille, providing the main route by which Senegalese people emigrated to France. Mambéty himself sailed on the *Ancerville* when he travelled to Marseille in 1968, and it is the same ship that Diouana takes to France in Sembene's *Black Girl*. By the time *Touki Bouki* was made, however, air travel was replacing liners and in 1973, the *Ancerville* was sold to the Chinese government.[81] In 1974, France would introduce a visa requirement for Senegalese visitors. This sea voyage was about to become a thing of the past, but *Touki Bouki*'s audience would have recognised the *Ancerville* as an icon of the postcolonial journey to Europe, with all its promise and dangers.

Matched with the melancholic sentiment that 'heartbreak lasts a lifetime' on the soundtrack (more on this song in Chapter 2), we tilt up the side of the *Ancerville*. Cargo is hoisted on board and a voice announces that the ship will leave Dakar at 4 pm. For the first time in the film, we encounter white people, in a montage of wealthy passengers sunning themselves on deck. A woman in a white minidress and a man in a captain's cap are unheard, as are a group of hard-faced middle-aged women wrapped in cardigans. Instead, we follow a conversation between two teachers: 'Our salaries are three times that of their teachers, but they don't eat as we do …

they're unrefined', and 'We never left Dakar. There's nothing to see in Senegal. Barren intellectually as well … African art is a joke.' This last speaker describes Senegalese people as 'big children' and asks rhetorically, 'What would we buy here? Masks?' This last comment also echoes *Black Girl*, in which an indigenous mask forms a central metaphor. The deck of the *Ancerville* hosts a sharp and satirical vignette of neocolonial attitudes among the white people in Senegal, who have not been the subject of the film but whose presence and ideologies still deform the postcolonial nation.

Down on the dock, a queue of young people line up to board the ship, including well-dressed men in suits, contrasting immediately with the white people's gross remarks. Whereas the white people were framed against blue skies, with endless space behind them, here we are cramped, the camera close to the crowd, and dock workers carrying sacks frequently cross the frame in extreme close-up. Anta walks up the gangway onto the ship but Mory, walking behind her, pauses and holds his chin ruminatively. This moment is the turning point of the film. Anta looks back down at Mory, still on the dock, and we cut to his memory of a lowing zebu in the slaughterhouse with the sound of the animal replaced with the ship's horn bellowing.

We return to Anta, who is often positioned on the extreme right-hand side of the frame, halfway to gone, and this time she walks completely off screen. Mory remains uncertain at the bottom of the gangplank, and we cut back to the zebu, now with the sounds of clanging knives, human shouts and booming echoes. When we cut back to Mory, he is running, the sky behind him and the ambient sounds of the abattoir still surrounding him. As he runs back along the quay, away from the *Ancerville*, a jazz-funk soundtrack emerges. We cut back to Anta, standing awkwardly on deck with her suitcase as Mory heads back to the city.

The film ends on the ambiguity of these choices. Anta stays on the ship, looking more uncertain and less full of swagger than before. She leans over the edge of the deck, chin in hand, and looks back towards Dakar and Mory. As she crosses the deck, we see the city behind her. Meanwhile, Mory has found the wreck of his motorbike and takes the broken zebu skull from the road. He sits down on a staircase on the rue Caillé, the impulse that propelled him off the ship seeming to have dissipated into stasis. The postman walks past him down the stairs and onto rue Henri Malan at the entrance of the docks. When the postman walks out of shot, we are left with

an image of the streets framing the port. We cut to the *Ancerville* crossing the frame, finally departing Dakar with Anta aboard, and then a wide shot of the ship moving out to sea. We flash back to the couple naked on Cap Manuel by the ocean, to a lengthy shot of a tiny sailboat at sea and finally all the way back to Mory as a child on his zebu. Mory has chosen Senegal and the land, Anta France and the sea, but neither of these journeys offers certainty.

Touki Bouki's ending has prompted a range of interpretations and it's notable that the western press often saw it as pessimistic. *Libération* compares the couple to human flares who end up consuming themselves, and *Le Monde* sees Mory as wandering like a lost soul.[82] French critics tended to depoliticise the film and didn't view Mory as making a deliberate decision to stay in Senegal. *Variety* characterises Mory's reason for leaving the *Ancerville* as 'an almost atavistic need to find a fetish', whereas 'the girl gets away'.[83] These accounts lean on romanticising the outlaw couple and in presenting Anta's choice as an escape; there is no space for the idea that going to France might not be the better option. More recent scholarship has viewed Mory's refusal as what Malini Guha calls 'the primary act of resistance' in the film.[84] For Anna Livia, 'Mory's refusal to board the ship thus reads like an answer to Diouana's suicide [in *Black Girl*]: a plea for life in Africa rather than death in France.'[85] Mory's choice is neither simplistic nor triumphant, as none of the problems of life in Senegal have gone away. But in the montage of ship and slaughterhouse, *Touki Bouki* forms what Walter Benjamin called a dialectical image, in which different times, places and objects suddenly fit into place to create a new and vivid understanding.[86] In a moment of brilliant clarity, Mory sheds a Eurocentric worldview.

The journey of *Touki Bouki* itself is this transformation of Dakar from origin to destination. The early generation of Senegalese film-makers thought about filming as a way of resignifying places that had only been captured by a violent colonial gaze, creating in Dakar a universal vision of the postcolonial city.[87] *Touki Bouki* certainly reimagines the space of Dakar and is entirely in love with its particularities; its shanty towns and its modernist arcades, its wrestling arenas and its oceanside corniche, its cafes and its market stalls. Moreover, this vision of the city makes space for a more diverse nation than official narratives would allow. As Sada Niang puts it, 'the film celebrates the town, its matriarchs, its credulous homosexuals, its carnivalesque political campaigns, the innocence of its children, its lazy youth'.[88] Mambéty returned from France, believing it to be more important to make films in Senegal. Reflecting on *Touki Bouki*'s dream of Europe, he said:

When I begin to dream of other places, to be obsessed by them to the point of becoming a stranger in my own country like Mory and Anta in *Touki-Bouki*, my natural instinct is to refuse the temptation. That is what has set the course of my life; I have always found it sad to be away from home.

He continues, 'It is as if I were born into an envelope, a lake from whose waters I never emerge. Every time I make a film, the creativity comes out of that original envelope. For me, filming is remembering.'[89] *Touki Bouki* might seem like a film about the desire to leave Africa for Europe but in the end, that desire and its refusal are part of a different journey.

assert Black cultural values as a refusal of the supposed universalism of European capitalism.[99] Reiland Rabaka terms it an 'insurgent idea', of continuing relevance to radical politics and art, and Gary Wilder sees in it a way of remaking the world that might speak to us today.[100]

The rich debate around Négritude contributed to making Senegal a centre of postcolonial Black thought. At the 1966 Festival mondial des arts nègres in Dakar, where Mambéty screened *Badou Boy*, Césaire gave a 'Lecture on African Art', in which he described two dangers: on the one hand, fawningly copying Europe and on the other, getting so stuck on finding an authentic African identity that art closes itself off from change.[101] This account of African art's role in the world sounds a much less essentialist note and suggests some of the creative directions that Mambéty would take. Mambéty has spoken of the 'influence of African culture on modern art', referring to Pablo Picasso's use of the African mask. 'That is the sort of contribution to cinematic writing that Africans can make ... What the masque nègre has done to advance modern art, it can do for cinematic writing.'[102] Rather than European artists appropriating African art, Mambéty imagines how African filmmakers might transform cinematic language through their own cultural heritage. Here, aesthetic forms do not indicate a nostalgic African essence but rather offer radical potential for artistic transformation.

For many Senegalese artists, Négritude was too closely associated with Senghor and an oppressive state vision of national culture. Ousmane Sembene rejected Négritude on Marxist grounds, but Mambéty was linked to a group of artists, writers and musicians who established the experimental Laboratoire Agit'Art.[103] The members of this group considered that Senghor's ideas of traditional African art were based on European ideas about Africa. They were open to influences from outside Africa but were opposed to adopting European standards of aesthetic value. In other words, they resisted the dogmas of both Eurocentrism and Négritude. As Ima Ebong notes, they deployed avant-garde forms not to critique Europe but to resist the Senegalese artistic establishment.[104] Mambéty's aesthetic emerges from this highly engaged milieu, thinking deeply about African and European cultural histories, both drawing from Négritude's intellectual energies and criticising its deficiencies.

I've taken some time to explore the context of these debates because it's useful to understand how steeped Mambéty was in questions of African aesthetics. Frameworks of authenticity have often been brought to bear on African films: critics ask whether African cinemas ought to draw on traditional worldviews, or whether it is inauthentic to engage with western forms. For many African film scholars, these debates reify and over-simplify African cultures. As David Murphy puts it, 'in my view, there is no "authentic" Africa, nor is there an "authentic" West'.[105] Manthia Diawara concurs, arguing that 'I do not believe that there is such a thing as an authentic African film language, whether it is defined in terms of commonalities arising from liberation struggles against colonialism and imperialism, identity politics, or Afrocentricity.'[106] Their rejection of ideas of authenticity and insistence on the cultural hybridity and plurality of African film aesthetics resonate with *Touki Bouki*. These conceptual frameworks do not come later but are the very material out of which Mambéty's own creativity was shaped. African cinema has a revolution to make, and to do so Mambéty at once draws on the plenitude of African aesthetic inheritances and refuses simplistic ideas of African essence. This perspective frames *Touki Bouki*'s aesthetics: its reimagining of oral culture, its modernist style and its creation of a global Black soundscape. With *Touki Bouki*, Mambéty imagines an African cinema navigating the shapes and histories of its own worldliness.

Oral tradition
Diawara writes that 'when African films are examined, one sees that all the directors resort in different ways to oral storytelling forms'.[107] Orality is the central category within which African cultural history

has been understood. As the great Malian writer Amadou Hampâté Bâ puts it,

> When we speak of African tradition or history we mean oral tradition; and no attempt at penetrating the history and spirit of the African peoples is valid unless it relies on that heritage of knowledge of every kind patiently transmitted from mouth to ear, from master to disciple, down through the ages.[108]

This idea of an oral tradition has been crucial for film-makers and critics seeking to claim an autochthonous film aesthetics for Africa. As the Négritude debates demonstrate, however, drawing from tradition is not simple: ideas of cultural heritage can be nostalgic and reactionary, or they can be turned towards political critique and artistic experiment in the present. Oral tales resist the Eurocentric idea that only writing constitutes historical knowledge and they form a living tradition, being 'constantly modernised so that they continue to reflect changing socio-cultural realities'.[109] *Touki Bouki*'s radical form derives in part from a desire to create modes of orality in and for modern cinema.

From the beginning, *Touki Bouki* tells its viewers that it won't be representing 'African tradition' in clichéd terms. If the opening scene of a child riding a zebu across a rural landscape seems to promise a pre-modern rural idyll, we are quickly disabused of this notion when the zebu are dispatched in a modern abattoir. And yet, the story does work with African narrative and cultural forms, all woven into the film's fictional world. Mory and Anta's plans for making money begin with a magical talisman or *gris-gris*, an object common in West African lore. After they have sex, the couple ride Mory's bike out of town, to an avenue of majestic baobab trees under which zebu graze. In this bucolic environment, they find a bright red bag by the river, which they recognise as containing someone's *gris-gris*. Anta warns Mory not to open it, but he does and pockets a good luck charm. Back in the Colobane market, this amulet prompts Mory to place a large bet, a gamble that does not work out for him.

Their next plan, to steal money from the wrestling arena, involves another encounter with *gris-gris*. Wrestling is associated with amulets and rituals, and matches often combine such animist beliefs with Islamic prayers. *Gris-gris* does not bring good luck in this episode either, as it turns out that the couple have accidentally stolen a case full of a wrestler's charms rather than the case full of money.

Their final plan to steal from Charlie does not involve any magical items, but its success leads the couple to celebrate via traditional cultural forms. After the robbery, as Mory stands in the back of Charlie's car, he imagines his victory in a voiceover proclaiming, 'Love me, I'm a wrestler anyway, hate me, I'm a wrestler anyway!' In Mory and Anta's fantasised visit to Aunt Oumy, she leads a traditional praise song, with a group singing, dancing and clapping as Oumy sings how Mory is 'the chosen one, our favourite friend'. When Mory dreams of being accepted by the community, he turns to these traditional figures of the wrestler and the praise singer, to the kind of collective belonging that no longer exists for him in Dakar.

The wrestler that Mory conjures sonically also thanks a *griot*, introducing the most revered figure in Senegalese oral culture: the *griot* is a storyteller and historian, central to the transmission of memory and construction of community.[110] *Griot* has also come to describe the cultural role of the African film-maker. Ousmane Sembene writes that 'The artist must in many ways be the mouth and ears of his people. In the modern sense, this corresponds to the role of the griot in traditional African culture.'[111] Describing the film-maker as a *griot* emphasises their social role, using storytelling both as a means to ensure the continuation of cultural histories and to speak out when others cannot about important political issues. The *griot* is a kind of court jester, licensed to speak truth to power.[112] Mambéty embraced the potential of the *griot*, saying that it 'for me means more than a storyteller; *griot* is a messenger of one's time, a visionary and the creator of the future'.[113] As a *griot*, the film-maker can shape cultural imaginaries, and for Mambéty, the visionary quality of the *griot* is part of his mission to reinvent cinema through African aesthetics. When the film-maker is a *griot* (a 'griauteur', in Murphy and Williams's hybrid coinage), oral culture doesn't consist of *what* is represented but in *how* film language is used.[114]

Oral culture depends on the spoken word, on embodied performance and rhetoric. How does the cinematic *griot* translate these ideas into the audiovisual language of film? A more direct equivalence might lead to a film oriented to speech, but *Touki Bouki* does not rely heavily on dialogue. Instead, the visionary quality of the *griot* plays across the entire formal repertoire of the screen. *Touki Bouki*'s narrative echoes the journey form of traditional Senegalese folktales, in which Mory undertakes a kind of initiatory quest. He begins in his village and undertakes a symbolic journey towards greater knowledge. In this interpretation, his final realisation that he wants to stay in Senegal represents the attainment of wisdom.[115] If we consider both Mory's and Anta's journeys, the narrative also has qualities of what Denise Paulme calls a 'mirror tale', in which two characters respond in opposite ways to the same challenges.[116] The journey is also circular, as the film begins and ends with the same shot. In the final sequence, we flashback to Anta and Mory lying on the ledge by Cap Manuel, then to the tiny sailboat on the ocean and finally back to Mory as a child on his zebu. We freeze-frame on this image of the past. For Emmanuelle Chérel, this circularity intimates an African worldview containing multiple epistemologies.[117] We have not superseded the world of the herder – it is still there, in parallel to the world of the modern city. As Melissa Thackway puts it, the oral tale sets up open-ended allegories for the audience to interpret.[118]

The *griot*'s tale is not linear but layered and digressive. *Touki Bouki* frequently veers from Mory and Anta's story, following minor characters who are not directly connected to the main plot but who add facets and multiple perspectives on its themes. For instance, we repeatedly return to a portly postman, first seen delivering letters from France in Anta's neighbourhood. A little later, we see him struggling to climb a steep verge and he returns when Mory is sitting confused on the steps outside the harbour. Another diversion features a white man who first appears in a tree and has come to Senegal to fulfil a 'savage' fantasy. Towards the end of the film, he takes Mory's motorbike and crashes it, ending up injured in an ambulance. What role does the European 'savage' play in this story of Africans

dreaming of Europe? It would be easy to see him as a rhyming European colonial fantasy of African authenticity, but the film never tells us directly who he is or what he is doing there.

Mambéty also draws from oral tales a mixture of imagination and the everyday, which Rolf Luapa describes as being simultaneously immersed in and detached from the real world.[119] When Mory is kidnapped by the university students, it is not quite fantastical, but it seems nightmarish or, in western terms, surreal. The students look wealthy, and they abuse their class position by lassoing Mory as if he were a zebu and tying him to the back of their jeep. It's a disconcerting act of dehumanisation, not least because we are never shown exactly what happens to Mory after they take him. Vlad Dima has even suggested that the entire story after the first twenty minutes of the film is a fantasy.[120] Although this interpretation is speculative, it is telling that the film is ambiguous enough for this reading to be possible. This fantastical quality does not distance the viewer from social realities, however, but renders hierarchies newly vivid through these disturbing visions. The *griot* has a unique licence to criticise the powerful, and Mambéty's satire of postcolonial Senegal emerges in these fantastical images.

Ideas of tradition are always contested. James Williams notes that by the 1980s, African film-makers turned to a more conservative mode of 'authenticity' (sometimes termed 'calabash cinema') that used traditional storytelling as a kind of heritage cinema.[121] Mambéty believed that African cultural traditions could offer something much more radical. For him,

> oral tradition is a tradition of images. What is said is stronger than what is written; the word addresses itself to the imagination, not the ear. Imagination creates the image and the image creates cinema, so we are in direct lineage as cinema's parents.[122]

In this, he resonates with Amadou Hampâté Bâ's expansive understanding of African culture. Bâ writes that

> African culture is not, then, something abstract that can be isolated from life. It involves a particular vision of the world, or rather a particular presence in the world – a world conceived of as a whole in which all things are linked together and interact.[123]

The *griot*'s imagination makes connections beyond the self. In *Touki Bouki*, orality is not a mode of being narrowly Senegalese or even African, neither cultural nationalism nor pan-Africanism, but rather it offers a way of seeing, a perspective onto the world.

Sonic transnationalisms

Sound, and especially music, forms a central part of *Touki Bouki*'s cinematic modernity. We open with the distinctive melody of the Fulani (or Peul) flute and across the film we hear Senegalese, French and African American musical styles. Mambéty's brother, Wasis – a significant musician who composed the soundtracks for his films – notes that 'Djibril is a musical film-maker. His cinema is musical because his ideas are musical.'[124] Sound contributes to the landscape of Dakar, from the early scene of Anta trying to work among the distractions of aeroplanes, sirens, crying babies, dogs barking and an imam's call all pressing in on her. In what Vlad Dima calls a 'sonic rack-focus', sound directs our attention and maps space.[125] The film often separates sound from image, from these quotidian off-screen dogs and babies to more disjunctive separations like Mory seeing the dying zebu matched to the sound of the ship's horn. Mbye Cham argues that sound for Mambéty is on an equal footing with the image, and the aesthetic autonomy of sound in *Touki Bouki* is nowhere more audible than in its inclusion of three singers: Aminata Fall, Mado Robin and Josephine Baker.[126] All three contribute to the film's liberated aesthetics, with Baker offering the most expansive example of an African sonic worldliness.

We have already touched on Aminata Fall, who plays Aunt Oumy and whose praise singing forms the centre of the fantasy sequence. Fall had been at the Daniel Sorano theatre company with Mambéty, and she would go on to act in *Le Franc* and *La Petite Vendeuse de soleil* as well as in other Senegalese films such as *Lambaaye* (1972) by Mahama Johnson Traoré and Bouna Medoune Seye's *Bandits cinéma* (1994). She is best known, however, as a singer of mbalax, a Senegambian genre that combines jazz, western

popular music and indigenous forms. She doesn't sing mbalax in *Touki Bouki* but her presence links Oumy's traditional praise song to what Babacar M'Baye has called the Afropolitan transnationalism of Fall's star persona.[127] Fall's singing style speaks to the transatlantic connections of Afro-diasporic music, from West African forms to Black American blues and jazz and back again. Fall famously said, 'When I hear that jazz comes from America, I'm outraged because jazz comes from Africa', and it's this interconnection of African and Afro-diasporic music that Mambéty plays with throughout *Touki Bouki*.[128]

The white French soprano Mado Robin forms a counterpoint to this transnational Black soundscape. Her version of 'Plaisir d'amour' is associated with the wealthy crowd at Charlie's house, introducing their Europeanised attitudes sonically. The song comes from the European classical tradition and was written in 1784; it has been recorded many times in more popular forms and the melody may be familiar to international audiences as the basis for Elvis Presley's 'Can't Help Falling in Love' from 1961. Robin herself died in 1960, so in the context of *Touki Bouki*, the song provides an oddly nostalgic echo of the colonial era. When we first hear it, 'Plaisir d'amour' implies the louche lifestyles and neocolonial social values of Charlie's friends, but the meaning shifts when the song repeats. In our first view of the *Ancerville*, the camera tilts up the side of the ship as we hear Robin singing the line 'heartbreak lasts a lifetime', along with the creaking of cargo ropes, followed by an announcement of the ship's departure time. The melancholic tone of Robin's voice now expresses the same warning that the zebu will offer to Mory – taking the ship will mean heartbreak and death.

Touki Bouki's most significant musical leitmotif, though, is Josephine Baker singing 'Paris, Paris, Paris', the same few lines of which recur throughout the film. Soon after Mory and Anta discuss leaving Senegal for the first time, they drive along on the motorbike as Baker sings the lines 'Paris, Paris, Paris, / C'est sur la Terre un coin de paradis'. The refrain repeats as we cut back and forth on the couple, eventually cutting to a wide shot of the bike passing among a row of baobab trees. The song recurs after the wrestling match, as Mory follows the stolen trunk around town and ruminates in voiceover about how he will succeed in Paris. As Anta leaves the travel agent triumphant with tickets to Marseille, it returns, and again as we enter the port. Its final reiteration comes when Anta sits alone on the deck of the *Ancerville*, looking less confident about this paradise to come. The song strikes us first as an ironic juxtaposition with the image, since the baobabs are an African landscape, far from Paris. Here, Baker could be heard as ventriloquising Mory and Anta's desire, their fantasy of Paris as a paradise on earth. In both form and content, though, this snippet of Baker's voice provokes other meanings.

Musical leitmotifs are common in oral performance, so this loop of Baker's song presents another way that *Touki Bouki* takes the forms of oral culture and transforms them into the language of cinema.[129] In this case, the extent of recurrence is extreme: rather than playing more of the song, the same two lines loop over and over again in what one review irritatedly calls 'an infernal repetition'.[130] The snippet is also edited in a disjunctive way. Alexander Fisher points out that each time it repeats, Baker is interrupting the time signature of the previous music, her voice coming in on the penultimate beat of the bar.[131] What was originally a smooth pop song becomes fractured and jarring. For Fisher, this sampling transforms Baker's French *chanson* into something closer to the polymetric form of West African music, in particular the *djembe* drum music that we hear in the wrestling arena.[132] By interrupting her French rhythm, Mambéty decolonises Baker's Paris.

This appropriation of Josephine Baker's music speaks to Mambéty's elaboration of a transnational Black modernity, for which Baker is a uniquely complex figure. The African American dancer had moved to Paris in 1925, where she became a sensation in *La Revue Nègre* and then a star in the all-Black revue at the Folies Bergère. In the 1920s, many Black Americans gravitated to Paris, which offered both an intellectual and artistic community and a limited escape from the racism of the US. Nonetheless, Baker was aware that her stardom depended on racist visual spectacle: she played to stereotypes of primitivism (one review referred to her 'magnificent animality') and her most famous performance was in a sexily revealing costume made of bananas.[133] The fashion for Black culture in Paris was linked to the avant-garde artists who used West African art as the basis for their new aesthetic language. Artists like Pablo Picasso, Fernand Léger, Henri Matisse and Le Corbusier were fans of Josephine Baker, seeing in her a link to both (a fantasised) African authenticity and to the potential of the modern. This admiration was at once sincere and fetishistic. As Karen Dalton and Henry Louis Gates Jr put it, 'Josephine Baker was primitivist-modernism on two legs, the cubists' *art nègre* in naked, human form.'[134]

Baker became the first Black woman to star in a major picture and her film career reveals a constant tension between the exoticism of her star vehicles and the space she carved out within them. In *La Sirène des tropiques/Siren of the Tropics* (Henri Étiévant and Mario Nalpas, 1927), she plays a very fictionalised version of her own story as a Caribbean woman who becomes a stage sensation in Paris. Each of her films locates her as some kind of exotic other: in *Zouzou* (Marc Allégret, 1934), starring opposite Jean Gabin, she is a Martinican who sings about Haiti, and in *Princesse Tam-Tam* (Edmond T. Gréville, 1935), she plays a Tunisian shepherdess who pretends to be a princess from a fictional country called Parador. She embodies an eroticised vision of Black femininity that, as Elizabeth Coffman argues, creates a spectacle of femininity and primativism that 'conflates the "problem" of women ... with "savages"'.[135] Baker's performances are at once complicit and transcendent. Her dances draw from West African and African American forms, and the films make visible the fetishistic desire of the white French audience for her Blackness.[136] In *Zouzou*, Gabin and a colleague watch Baker dance, her body outlined in a giant silhouette cast behind her. In the same film, she performs in a golden birdcage, clad in a revealing feathery tulle costume that bespeaks both elegant glamour and the bestialised

Josephine Baker sings in a golden cage in *Zouzou* (1934)

Black body. Although the racism of these films is well documented, Anne Anlin Cheng asks instead 'what would it mean to see Baker not as an example of but as a fracture in the representational history of the Black female body?'[137]

Touki Bouki takes up exactly this potential. Like the French modern artists, Mambéty is also searching for a new aesthetic vocabulary but one that doesn't replicate the colonial logic in which Baker could only embody an uncontaminated primitivism. By using her singing voice but not her image, *Touki Bouki* refuses the over-visibility of her Blackness. (Think also of how differently Anta inhabits her body. She is nothing like a misogynoir spectacle of erotic alterity, rather articulating a liberated vision of Black womanhood.) *Touki Bouki*'s use of Baker also flips the transnational quality of her stardom. Elizabeth Ezra notes that 'Baker's enormous popularity owed much to her cosmopolitan identity: she could evoke Africa, the Caribbean, the United States, and France, by turns or all at once as the occasion required.'[138] But where Baker's French films conflated various non-white identities in a colonial cosmopolitanism,

Mambéty rewrites Baker into the trajectories of the Black Atlantic. Like Aminata Fall, Baker performed at the Dakar Festival des arts nègres in 1966. In *Touki Bouki*, she voices a transnational Black modernity that far exceeds the colonial limitations of 'Paris'.

Modernism

For Mambéty, African aesthetics is anything but inward-looking, and in *Touki Bouki* he brings a particular African viewpoint to bear on the histories and potentials of world cinema. Formal strategies like repetition, fragmentation and editing out of chronology describe some of the ways that the film can be compared to European art cinema and especially the French New Wave. Anny Wynchank outlines a slew of such comparisons, from the repetitions of Anta running down the hill that evokes *L'Année dernière à Marienbad/Last Year at Marienbad* (Alain Resnais, 1961) to the freeze-frame of the final shot that recalls *Les Quatre cent coups/The 400 Blows* (François Truffaut, 1959).[139] The mode of production is also similar, with limited economic and technical resources leading film-makers to shoot in the street, with natural light, some non-professional actors and so forth. These comparisons are not inaccurate, but they risk reproducing a colonial framework of thought in which European cinema constitutes an origin and Africa merely a copy. This attitude is implied in Wynchank's assessment that *Touki Bouki* is 'an African illustration of the French New Wave films'.[140] Wes Felton has tried to complicate this picture by considering how Francophone African film-makers also influenced the French New Wave. From Vieyra's filming of *Afrique sur Seine* (1955) in Paris, African film-makers were, in his words, 'caught in the undertow' of French cinematic modernism.[141]

As the Négritude debates demonstrate, the stakes of western aesthetic influence were well understood by Mambéty and his Senegalese peers. Writing in *Le Soleil*, Pierre Souillac wonders how those critics who rejected *Touki Bouki* as European in style would define an African mode of filming a landscape, a human figure or colours.¹⁴² For Souillac and very much so for Mambéty, French cinema does not get to own formal experimentation. After all, if *Touki Bouki* tells a story about the perils of being seduced by a dream of Paris, it is hardly likely that its director would himself be seduced by French cinematic form. As Heather Snell puts it, 'The disappointment of the critic who finds that the African film is too "Western" is matched only by the desire for Paris that permeates Mambéty's vision of Senegal as a corrupt, neocolonial failure.'¹⁴³ Such fantasies of the other are always caught in a colonial relationality.

Indeed, *Touki Bouki*'s character of the white primitive can be seen as a satirical nod to this colonialist desire to find an authentic African way of being. We first encounter him sitting in a tree, clad in animal skins and cawing like a crow. He is a ridiculous figure, but he also confuses Anta and causes her to crash, in a sequence that veers suddenly into a subjective camera position from the point of view of Anta's bike. As is often the case, eyelines don't match. Anta looks the 'wrong' way, and we cut unexpectedly to a vertiginous ground-level view moving rapidly through grass. Saïdou Alceny Barry describes a camera that dances between twirling and

explosion, and this sequence exemplifies the film's sudden switches of perspective.[144] Mambéty worked with Georges Bracher, a French director of photography who was based in Dakar and who, with his photographer wife Maya, had strong connections across Senegal's film culture. The couple also collaborated with Sembene, Safi Faye and Ben Diogaye Bèye, and with the American photographer Eliot Elisofon. Mambéty makes use of Bracher's 'freewheeling style and observational camera eye', breaking down his open cinematography into what Kemal Ndiaye calls the film's 'kneaded, broken, twisted rhythms'.[145] Rather than seeing *Touki Bouki* as copying the French New Wave, it is more accurate to think of Mambéty as using a wide array of cinematic techniques in the creation of an African cinematic modernity.

Ideas of cinematic modernism can't simply be imported from Europe to Africa, because modernity does not have the same meanings for formerly colonised countries. As Melissa Thackway succinctly puts it, 'it has to be acknowledged that modernity has been experienced under entirely different terms and conditions in Africa, and thus has generated quite different "modernist" aesthetics. If we are to use the term "modernism", therefore, it needs to be "decolonised".'[146] Modernist styles of art have often been rejected in African contexts as both tainted with European colonialism and as elitist and exclusionary – we see this also in critiques of literary modernists like Wole Soyinka.[147] And yet, cinematic realism is also a tainted inheritance for African film-makers. Supposedly neutral documentary was the main way in which African people had been represented during the colonial period, and the racist nature of those films destroyed any faith in realism's truth status. In Rachel Gabara's words, 'if nonfiction films have lied about you, you are not likely to believe and repeat clichés of documentary objectivity and form'.[148] Mambéty reinvents both documentary realism and modernist styles, turning newsreel footage of Omar Bongo's state visit to Dakar into a fantasy parade and situating 'aesthetic rupture' in the lifeworlds of the postcolonial city.[149]

These forms come together in the wrestling stadium, where Mambéty films his actors at a real event. The images have a documentary force as the camera ranges across the competitors and the audience, but the editing deconstructs any sense of objectivity. We first hear *djembe* drums on the soundtrack as the camera pans across drums in the arena, but these drums are not being played. There is a temporal gap in which the soundtrack is located in the future. We cut to empty bleachers and then back to drums, which are now being played by musicians. The offset sound and image prompt us to pay attention to the traditional drumming as something other than background, to hear the music and see the musicians as a culturally resonant presence. Together with Fall, Baker and the jazz-funk that accompanies Mory's flight from the *Ancerville*, they create what James Genova calls 'a counterhegemonic image-Africa that claimed a place for African self-representation within the international field of motion picture production'.[150] *Touki Bouki*'s audiovisual modernism is not merely a set of formal references. It is inextricably blended with its orality, so that the film's expressive montage, its non-linear narration and its hallucinatory compositions simultaneously create an African cinematic style and a worldly one.

3 Embodiment

Touki Bouki films bodies in strikingly bold ways, from its frank depictions of sexuality and desire to the violence of its animal deaths. It contains an audacious sex scene that's rare in African cinemas of the period, as well as several scenes of nudity. It prominently features a gay character, and its protagonists present in ways that often seem dissident in terms of gender or sexuality. Its bodily representation also extends beyond the human with memorable scenes centring on zebu and goats, to say nothing of its title, the hyena's journey. These animals are both allegorical and material, echoing the power dynamics of the human characters but also powerfully speaking of their own lives. Human and non-human animals are often compared, as in the crisis point when Mory links the line of people embarking on the *Ancerville* to the zebu entering the slaughterhouse. Even in less fraught moments, though, it's worth paying attention to how the film looks at bodies.

In an early scene, Anta cuts across a group of women washing clothes. She is unconcerned with their conventional feminine labour, but the film lingers on the women. In a series of shots around the water tap, a child looks towards the camera awkwardly and a woman crosses the frame, smiling. 'If you want water, you'd better listen,' barks the man in charge. The camera follows one woman as she walks away with a water container on her head, framed from the waist down, focusing on her swaying backside. In the next shot, another woman looks mischievously towards the camera. Although we could read a male gaze in the focus on women's bodies, the camera's interest is not conventionally fetishistic. The women are figures of labour, less powerful than the men who oversee this work but resistant to their authority. Their bodily gestures – the smile, the sway, the looks – all suggest an awareness shared between

TOUKI BOUKI | 73

camera and subject that excludes the officious and demanding men. A rhyming scene takes place at the wrestling arena, when the camera once again looks admiringly at labouring bodies. This time, the bodies are male, as the semi-naked wrestlers face off before the watching eyes of the crowd. As well-dressed men and women in the audience look on, one wrestler, also viewed from behind, swings

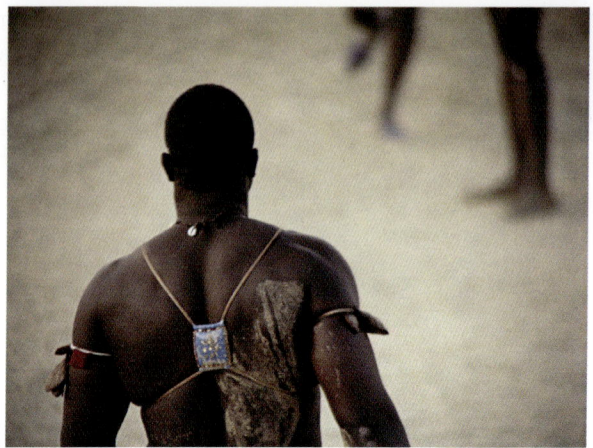

his muscular torso back and forth as he warms up. The shot is reminiscent of the water-carrying woman; another gaze at part of a body in elegantly swaying motion, a person working but also moving in time. The gaze here might be read as homoerotic. We are watching the same spectacle as the audience, and yet Mambéty's camera asks us to focus not on sport but on corporeality.

Throughout the film, Mambéty asks us to pay attention to bodies, to consider their eroticism, their labour, their radical energies and often transgressive potentials. Giuseppe Gariazzo describes *Touki Bouki* as 'A body-cinema that shuns conventions and beautiful images, that immerses itself in otherness, that makes its body a place of mutation and risk, in infinite contact with death and life.'[151] The abattoir scene at the very beginning of the film jolts us into this sense of bodies as fragile, and some critics have emphasised the exercise of power over the bodies of those who, like the zebu, cannot protect themselves.[152] And yet, alongside the violence, *Touki Bouki* insistently locates queer pleasure in bodies and it intertwines an anticolonial critique with dissident forms of sexuality and gender. Think of Anta in her French drag, exuding elite neocolonial lady energy in the travel agency and demonstrating how gender presentation is intimately linked to geopolitical power. Black feminist scholars such as Zakiyyah Iman Jackson and Rizvana Bradley have interrogated the significance of corporeality, gender and violence for Black art, so this politics of embodiment is linked to the liberated aesthetics of the previous chapter.[153] Across *Touki Bouki*, bodies signify as figures of resistance.

Seeing sex

When Anta runs down to the foot of the cliffs looking for Mory, what follows is a sex scene at once intense and experimental. Anta first leans against the cliff face, seemingly alone. The sequence does not cut to a wide shot of the space around her but instead begins to fragment and disperse into an increasingly sensual montage. Shots of Anta viewed from behind are interspersed with the tide running into a narrow pebble beach, the zebu horns from Mory's motorcycle sitting on the rocks and the Dogon cross that decorates the back of the bike. These fragments of his bike tell us that Mory is here, but we do not see him. Instead, we hear Anta's breathing, closely miked, layered with the sounds of zebu lowing and a boat's horn. Anta walks into shot with the Dogon cross visible beside her. She takes her

shirt off, revealing her naked torso, and then sinks below the frame line. Her nudity is surprising but also matter of fact, not a striptease. As her body vanishes from view, it is the soundtrack that discloses the scene's sexual tempo. The camera begins to trace the shoreline as waves spill over rocks, along with the intimately proximate sound of Anta's increasingly ragged breathing. We cut back to her hand on the cross coming in and out of focus. She catches her breath as a plume of spray flies into the air, followed by smaller waves breaking, then we cut back to her hand slowly loosening and disengaging from the cross. After another shot of white, foaming eddies, we cut to a shot of smoother seas with a small boat sailing by. Mory registers for the first time as a voice-off, saying, 'There's a boat leaving tomorrow, let's take it', and we cut to our first and only view of the couple lying naked together in front of the ocean.

This is indisputably a sex scene but very little is seen, and critics have debated how to understand it. The conventional view is that African cinemas avoid direct representations of sex, both because of dominant social values that are sexually conservative and because cinema is seen as a space for public conversation, not the depiction of private desire.[154] Françoise Pfaff takes this approach, arguing that 'eroticism ... is indeed scarce or at best generally quite benign in most sub-Saharan African films because of their sociopolitical nature'.[155] She calls the scene 'the most innovative and puritanical love encounter of African cinema', taking it straightforwardly as a scene that is too repressed to show sex visually.[156] But is this lengthy and lyrical exploration of female pleasure really puritanical? The soundtrack places us intimately close to Anta's body, attuned to her mouth and her chest as she breathes. Her fingers grip and release the Dogon cross in ecstasy and the montage of ocean waves tracks the temporality of her pleasure in some detail. Far from being puritanical, the scene lingers deliciously on Anta's orgasm.

It's no surprise that several critics have disagreed with Pfaff. Kenneth Harrow argues that *Touki Bouki* 'broke the relatively prudish conventions hitherto followed by African film-makers in the representation of sexual desire', and Greg Thomas rebuffs the charge of puritanism, saying that it's 'hardly religious, British, or repressive'.[157] For Thomas, the scene expands the potential of cinematic eroticism beyond voyeurism, and this expansion helps us see how sex fits into the film's larger project of aesthetic liberation. Sex is not separate from politics for *Touki Bouki*, and this scene does not exist merely to provide insight into Anta's inner life. From the beginning, Anta's relationship with Mory is depicted as a source of conflict. Her mother considers him to be a ne'er-do-well who reflects badly on Anta's femininity. The Marxist students also hate Mory and accuse Anta of caring about 'screwing' more than about politics. By enjoying sex with Mory, Anta actively rejects both the conventional standards of female behaviour demanded by her family and the narrow and sexist vision of radical politics espoused by the students. The scene counters patriarchal vision by centring Anta's experience of sex.[158] It also places her embodied experience of sex and gender at the heart of *Touki Bouki*'s critique of neocolonialism.

Queer bodies

Although *Touki Bouki* centres on an opposite-sex relationship, its transgression of representational norms around gender and sexuality, along with its depiction of homosexuality, give the film an insistently queer feeling. David Murphy and Patrick Williams claim that it is 'tempting to read a "queer" aesthetic into Mambéty's work, that is, the exploration and celebration of marginal, nonconformist identities (rather than of homosexuality *per se*)'.[159] The same affection for social outsiders and postcolonial 'delinquency' that made *Touki Bouki* controversial with Senegalese audiences leads it off the path of gender and sexual normativities. Homophobic voices often claim that queerness is western and leverage African 'tradition' to impose oppressive gender roles and to violently foreclose on queer African lives.[160] But homophobia is also a violent colonial inheritance, determining ways of being and modes of visuality from which *Touki Bouki* overtly divests. Spaces for queer African cinema have been limited but, as Lindsey Green-Simms notes, cinematic resistance to heteronormativity can take the forms of 'loving, touching, fighting, running away, staying put, staying quiet, taking refuge in customary practices, and dreaming of otherworldly possibilities'.[161] *Touki Bouki*'s queerness goes beyond an affiliation with marginality, placing resistant visions of sex, gender and embodiment at the heart of the film's radicality.

Anta's gender presentation is unconventional from the first time we see her. Her mother and the woman buying vegetables are both dressed in traditional headscarves and *boubous* but Anta wears trousers and a shirt, her short hair uncovered. She does not dress like the other women and nor does she behave like them: she bursts into the scene, arguing with the customer and angering her mother. Several critics of the film refer to her as a 'garçonne' or tomboy, a term that has often connoted a queer woman, and Anta's costume and posture play with masculinity.[162] We've already noted how she undresses in the sex scene, a complicated moment in which she reveals her body but disrobes with an insouciance that refuses gestures of feminine modesty or striptease. At Charlie's party, she wears her shirt entirely unbuttoned, in a way usual only for men,

so that her breasts are almost revealed. This moment of cross-dressing coincides with her stealing from the bag of one of Charlie's wealthy guests: her delinquency goes hand in hand with a resistance to gender norms. She wears a dress only when in disguise at the wrestling match – even the lilac trouser suit she adopts to leave for France consists of pieces stolen from Charlie and transformed into a chic female masculinity.

Mory also cuts a queer figure, his rangy body often the object of an eroticised gaze. When the couple first go to the wrestling stadium, he sits spreadeagled on the bleachers, legs wide apart and arms thrown behind him in a cool, James Dean-like pose. The shot emphasises his corporeality with quite a queer look at his tight trousers and T-shirt. Later, he throws his clothes off and stands naked in the back of Charlie's stolen car in a moment that again links delinquency and bodily liberation. Anna Livia sees this naked parade as containing a gay subtext and 'a warning that we cannot align the butch, short-haired Anta and the superbly naked Mory with Western couples like Bonnie and Clyde'.[163] When the couple go to the beach at Ngor, Mory reclines on the sand wearing orange trunks. In an arresting composition, we see his upper body, head bowed,

with golden sand the exact same colour as his necklace adhering to his face and torso. The grains of sand decorate his skin like glitter, turning the Dakar beach momentarily into a stage or a disco. He looks up towards the sky and smiles, holding this pose for several seconds. Mory's body, in an image that is beautiful, aestheticised, but also delicate in its eroticism, illuminates a mode of image-making that resists both the colonial and patriarchal gaze. In such moments, *Touki Bouki* gestures towards new forms of queer African visuality.

The film's most visibly queer character is Charlie, a rich gay man from whom Mory and Anta steal money and clothes. We pull back from a familiar shot of the sea foam to a swimming pool, in which Charlie is reclining in a pedalo with a young man. He tells his companion to scram and invites Mory into the pedalo, then shoos Anta away to join the women. The scene is decadent: bored-looking women lounge on deckchairs smoking, while a man in a bathrobe casts a fishing net into the pool in a hipster pastiche of labour. The scene establishes homosexuality as indolence, akin to Karl Schoonover's description of cinematic queerness as looking like wasted time, in which 'queers luxuriate while others work'.[164] Charlie, luxuriating in a fluffy white bathrobe, is also overly familiar,

petting at Mory in the pedalo and then manhandling him up the stairs towards the house.

Inside, we hear Charlie's voice off screen telling Mory to make himself at home while Charlie showers. He flirts with Mory and asks about Anta, saying that he's not jealous of her 'but there's a big difference between hens and goats'. He uses an animal metaphor to distinguish men from women, imagining desire for men through the voracious goat. He instructs Mory to strip and offers to rub his back. The exchange sets Charlie up as clueless, since Mory is stealing from him while he showers, but the scene also clearly implies that Mory has been there before and that he is familiar with Charlie's hospitality and his bedroom. Have their previous encounters been transactional? Is Mory one of Charlie's 'boys'? Mory's participation in this queer subculture echoes an encounter with a policeman in the Plateau. The cop stops Mory on his bike and Mory responds with recognition: 'What a surprise, brother, you're a cop!' He relates that after the cop left the other night, the place they had been was raided by the police. The policeman quickly insists that 'we've never met' and tells him to leave and not mess up his career. Queer culture on the down-low links Mory, Charlie and figures of state authority.

When Charlie emerges from the shower to discover that Mory has stolen from him, he sits down at his desk to call the police. A long take discloses a highly decorative *mise en scène*: Charlie is surrounded by a vase of pink flowers, a glass lamp, a fertility totem, a powder-blue telephone and a large sunflower lampshade on the desk, on top of a blue-and-white patterned tablecloth. On the wall, a large black-and-white wall hanging depicting various animals is partially covered by a retro Art Nouveau poster. In the midst of this 'lushly queer domestic nest' sits Charlie, shirtless against an orange pillow.[165] The decor is what I have elsewhere called 'pretty', an aesthetic that uses colourful props and decorative detail to overturn the masculine, Eurocentric preference for simplicity in favour of a queer visual plenitude.[166] The scene becomes more camp when Charlie speaks to a certain Division Commander Djibril Diop, played by the director himself. Charlie flirts with Commander Diop, addressing him in familiar French, reproaching him for not coming over before, and inviting him to come and take down his statement in person.

The character of Charlie has prompted much debate among critics of the film. Some, like Kenneth Harrow, find the representation to be homophobic, considering that it 'produces a familiar trope of gayness as unnatural, and even worse, as reflective of the corrupt elements in the society and government'.[167] It's easy to agree with this assessment, since Charlie is there to be duped by our heroes, and the film invites the viewer to laugh at his French affectations and his flirtation with Commander Diop. Charlie's advances are heavy-handed, even predatory, and his proximity to state power speaks to the cosy world of the postcolonial elite. And yet, this is not the only way to read Charlie and his milieu. The film makes a queer subculture visible, part of the urban weft of Dakar, and if Charlie loses out in this encounter, his phone conversation provides a sequel that doesn't leave him as a victim. Viewed without context, Charlie can seem like a stereotype, but his effeminacy forms the central term in a queer visual register that traverses the film. James Williams sees Mambéty as 'a "queer uncle" of African modernism', and Greg Thomas finds throughout *Touki Bouki* 'trickster performances of sex and gender against the hegemonic logic of sex and gender itself, under colonialism or neocolonialism'.[168] Mory and Anta's trickster embodiment turns sex and gender into a queer refusal of colonial logic.

The hyena's journey

The lives of animals in *Touki Bouki* exist in the same moral universe as those of humans. Animal scholars have criticised the tendency of cinema to use non-human animals merely as metaphors with which to illuminate human stories, and it's certainly true that the film mobilises animals in its Eisensteinian montage. When we see a zebu in the slaughterhouse matched to the sound of the *Ancerville*, this juxtaposition tells us something about postcolonial migration rather than something about zebu. Contrarily, the opening abattoir scene is powerful on its own terms as a documentation of how humans dispose of the lives of other creatures. We could interpret the scene in relation to rural life, halal slaughtering practices or other aspects of human culture, but the material force of the zebus' fear and the life force draining from their necks stays with us beyond any contexts.

Sada Niang speaks of the 'spiritual density' of the film's animals, and for him this idea separates those who see zebu, goats and humans as things to be exploited from those who, like Mory with his precious zebu skull, have a deep connection to the land and its inhabitants.[169] This spiritual density complicates the idea that animal metaphors are wholly anthropocentric: for *Touki Bouki*, animals express an interconnectivity of life force, or *nyama*, that draws from West African oral tradition and resists a colonial nature/culture binary.

The most prominent non-human animal in *Touki Bouki* is not corporeal at all, because the hyena of the film's title is never seen on screen. Who or what is this titular hyena? West African oral culture is full of animal tales, such as the *Contes d'Amadou Koumba*, which feature a hyena alongside tales of lions, chickens, toads, dogs and a wily hare named Leuk.[170] Within this folkloric bestiary, the hyena has a bad reputation, being associated with 'greediness ... aggressiveness, trickiness of a particularly crude sort ... and often plain stupidness'.[171] The hyena is immoral and dirty, stupid and dangerous, representing the worst qualities of the animal world.[172] This negative view is echoed in western beliefs about the hyena, dating all the way from Aristotle, who believed them to be hermaphroditic, cowardly and treacherous.[173] As Stephen Glickman points out, we can see the bad reputation of hyenas portrayed in popular films like *The Lion King* (Rob Minkoff and Roger Allers, 1994), but the oddity of these animals being viewed as ambiguously gendered suggests that for Mambéty, they might be something other than simple villains.[174]

Who is the hyena in *Touki Bouki*? The most obvious answer would be Mory, since he is the protagonist who undertakes a journey. And yet, Mory is not stupid, dangerous or cowardly. He is admittedly somewhat immoral, but he's not a villain or an anti-hero. We can think of Mory as the hyena, but to do so we must reframe what the hyena signifies. Olivier Barlet sees Mory as a trickster figure whose schemes and dreams enable Anta to leave, and Thomas picks up on the perverse qualities of the hyena myth, seeing ideas of hermaphrodism, androgyny and sexual deviation as 'the stuff of Mambéty'.[175] Thus he sees Mambéty offering a positive account of hyenas in *Touki Bouki* inasmuch as they stand for non-conformity or a social marginality that is not merely negative. In an interview, Mambéty implies that Africans had to take on the role of the hyena, stalking the lion of colonialism, waiting for it to lie down in weakness. Or, the hyena might be read as the myth of Europe, via whiteness as a dream that stalks Africans.[176] Along these lines, Niang argues that Mory is not the hyena, but the title would be better translated as a journey that is hyena-ised.[177] These ambivalent interpretations remediate the psychological legacies of colonialism through African oral culture.

If the hyena is an imaginary presence across *Touki Bouki*, embodied animals play a key role in the film's cinematic modernity. Right after Mory is captured by the students, we cut to a shot of a goat and two unidentified people grabbing the animal. The captured goat is crosscut with the students holding Mory, then another location is introduced as we cut to Anta running down a path by the cliffs. An insistent metallic percussive sound gets louder as we cut back and forth across these spaces. The relationship between these shots is unclear – the captured goat parallels Mory's situation but is the editing only metaphoric or are they contiguous in space and time? The couple hold the goat down over a metal door and slit its throat. We cut to Anta, looking down at the ground, the motorbike visible beside her. The editing implies that she is looking down at the goat, but we will later discover that she is not. We might also be suspicious about the appearance of the bike in this shot because, if these were parallel edits, the bike should be back with the students. The scene creates a disjunctive and disorienting effect, in which we feel the violence and anxiety that swirls around all three figures (Mory, Anta, goat) but cannot easily locate them in relation to one another.

The sequence continues to cut back and forth from Anta to the dying goat, its blood bright red against the equally vibrant yellow door. Anta takes off her shirt to reveal her breasts, this unexpected

nakedness providing a sharp contrast with the violent intimacy of the dying goat. From a close-up of the dead goat's throat, we pull out to reveal Aunt Oumy flaying the animal. Anta skids down the hill to the outdoor cafe where Oumy is working, bringing two of these spaces together. Just as we might think that the disparate scenes will coalesce, however, the film undercuts its own coherence. We cut to the goat, now alive and bleeding once again, a temporal glitch in which the goat's impossible resurrection provides a corporeal marker of time out of joint. From the goat, we cut rapidly to waves crashing against the rocks and to Anta, jumping once again over a wall in a shot we have seen before. The film's temporality repeats, fragmenting and recursively doubling and tripling Anta's trajectory down the cliff path. A shot of birds in the sky is followed by the goat, dying once again, and water eddying around rocks. The montage is increasingly associative and abstract, as is the soundtrack, which intertwines bird cries, Oumy's laugh, the goat bleating, and distorted and reverberating electronic sound effects. The goat's death marks a point of finitude that the film uses to articulate its non-linearity: we understand the film's temporality in and through animal mortality.

This scene exemplifies how Mory is associated with zebu and goats and how embodiment binds together human and non-human animals. On the *Ancerville*, Mory fears becoming like a zebu led to the slaughter – the film repeatedly associates him with sacrificed animals and his resistance is a refusal to become this kind of compliant body, sacrificed to the appetites of society. The hyena is smarter than that, and if he doesn't have the strength to attack in daylight, he knows how to choose his moment. The zebu's journey ends in one place, the abattoir, but Mory ultimately refuses a one-way trip. The film's connection of human and animal exploitation is another form of postcolonial critique, since the hierarchy of human over animal is part of a colonial (and religious) worldview. *Touki Bouki* is not advocating animal rights in a western sense, but it understands the lives and spirits of animals as intertwined with those of humans, and as intrinsic to an African worldview.

4 Afterlives

Touki Bouki resonates across world cinema. We can trace its afterlives first in two quasi sequels, one directed by Djibril Diop Mambéty himself, almost twenty years later, and the other by his niece, Mati Diop. Mambéty's own *Hyenas*, made in 1992, forms an attenuated sequel, although it is adapted from *Der Besuch der alten Dame*/*The Visit* (1956), by Swiss playwright Friedrich Dürrenmatt. It forms the second part of an unfinished trilogy about power set in the neighbourhood of Colobane in Dakar. In *Hyenas*, we are presented again with a woman who left Africa and her boyfriend who stayed. Mambéty said of the film that

> I began to make *Hyènes* when I realized I absolutely had to find one of the characters in *Touki-Bouki*, which I had made twenty years before. This is Anta, the girl who had the courage to leave Africa and cross the Atlantic alone … Linguère Ramatou is also marginalized, because she is exactly the same person who crossed the Atlantic to go to Europe in *Touki-Bouki*.[178]

The protagonists in *Hyenas* are not literally the same characters as Anta and Mory but they imagine what might become of people like them, decades later.

Mory's equivalent, Draaman Drameh, has become a respected pillar of the community, owning a local cafe and general store, but the return of Linguère Ramatou throws his life and that of Colobane into disarray. Linguère has become a wealthy woman, and she returns in triumph, bestowing riches on the townspeople. There is a catch, however. Linguère was pregnant when she left and Draaman denied that the child was his, preferring to marry for social status. Linguère was forced to become a prostitute in the West. Her wealth was hard-won, and she is bitter. She makes the town an offer:

With Linguère and Draaman, *Hyenas* imagines a couple like Anta and Mory, many years later

kill Draaman and she will give them vast riches. This moral dilemma sets the stage for a dark fairy tale about western consumer capitalism, African modernity and human greed. The townspeople all express disgust at Linguère's offer but slowly, Draaman notices people with new shoes, fridges and air conditioners. The desire for commodities wins out over human values. *Hyenas* returns to the themes of *Touki Bouki* with a violent difference. Now, the globalised world has come to Africa and its effects are destructive.

As in *Touki Bouki*, though, Senegalese society is also criticised, and transnational economic contexts intersect with gender politics. From Linguère's perspective, the people of Colobane were all complicit in ruining the life of a young woman with their hypocritical and sexist moral code. Her relationship with Draaman held no consequences for him, only for her. The smooth surface of Colobane society continues by expelling troublesome women like Linguère and exposing them to suffering in the West. Where Anta and Charlie found space to resist normativity, Linguère was not so fortunate. Nor are the two genderqueer figures who are dragged out, captured in nets, to bear witness to the lies told about Linguère.[179] Linguère has none of Anta's youthful optimism but her return, surrounded by a transnational guard of women including a Japanese police officer and three women in elaborate Fulani costumes, draped in jewellery, creates a compelling visual spectacle of feminine authority.

Like *Touki Bouki*, *Hyenas* is set wholly in Dakar and uses this perspective to speak about the world. There are other echoes, beginning with the recurrence of the hyena in the film's title. In both films, the identity of the titular hyenas is ambiguous and layered. Linguère might be a hyena who lies in wait in the dark until her stronger opponent is tired and weakened. But the people of Colobane are also hyenas, greedy and stupid people who double-cross Draaman and eventually surround and kill him. Finally, global capitalism is a hyena that stalks Senegal. Linguère is described as 'richer than the World Bank', and the international system of debt and finance hangs over the little people of Colobane like a spectre.[180] *Hyenas* elaborates a more cynical vision of Africa's place in the world than *Touki Bouki*, but it remains deeply committed to the beauty and potential of the continent. Mansour Diouf, the actor who plays Draaman Drameh, describes *Hyenas* as 'a beautiful story, a modern tale of Senegalese history, indeed of Africa, of the world as a whole'.[181] This rapid expansion from Senegal to Africa to the world captures Mambéty's approach to cinema; grounded in Senegal, engaged in African culture and always worldly.

Another twenty years after *Hyenas*, Mambéty's niece Mati Diop made *Mille soleils*/*A Thousand Suns* (2013), an experimental docu-fiction that traces the actors who played Mory and Anta, all these years later. The film begins with Magaye Niang herding zebu in Dakar, like his child equivalent did in the opening scene of *Touki Bouki*. Magaye did remain in Senegal just like Mory, but he is not really a zebu herder, the first indication that Diop's film is a mix of fiction and fact. Myriam Niang, the actor who played Anta, also left Senegal, a parallel with the film that Diop reflects on throughout *A Thousand Suns*. In her version, Myriam is a mysterious figure, not seemingly played by Niang herself and glimpsed only fleetingly striding naked through the snows of Alaska. The mix of fantasy and realism that defines *Touki Bouki* is expanded here, combining art cinematic ambiguity with the resistance to documentary realism characteristic of postcolonial African film.

Diop has returned frequently to stories of young people leaving Senegal for Europe. One of her early short documentaries is *Atlantiques* (2009), in which young men talk about the hopelessness of economic prospects at home and their foreknowledge of their own likely death at sea. Her first feature, 2019's *Atlantique/Atlantics*, turns that reality into a ghost story, in which the spirits of drowned men possess their girlfriends in Dakar. *Atlantics* frames the lives of these young people in terms of an oceanic haunting that encompasses a long history from the transatlantic slave trade through colonial and postcolonial exploitation of Africa by Europe. In *Atlantics*, it is the boyfriend, Souleiman, who leaves, and the future belongs to Ada, who stays. *Touki Bouki*'s story of leaving and staying is part of Diop's inheritance.

Returning to *A Thousand Suns*, Diop brings together the generation of Anta and Mory with the young people in Dakar protesting the government in the present day. Magaye takes a taxi to a celebratory outdoor screening of *Touki Bouki*, where he will

A screening of *Touki Bouki* in *A Thousand Suns* (2013)

be feted on stage. The taxi driver, played by popular musician and activist Djily Bagdad, argues with Magaye about politics, insisting that the radical movements of the 1960s and 70s failed to deliver democracy or improve living conditions. 'What have you achieved with your struggles?' he demands. 'What have you left us as a legacy?' At the screening, we see the older Magaye silhouetted in front of the image of his younger self running away from the *Ancerville* as Anta looks off the deck (and out of the screen) towards him. The sequence movingly condenses the many gaps between then and now, between documentary and fiction, between youth and age, and between postcolonial hope and political disappointment. James Williams sees the film as exploring cinematic memory and heritage, using fiction film itself as an archive in what he dubs 'a veritable case study of film genealogy and cinematic succession'.[182] Diop's film reflects on the failures of the anticolonial generation in Senegal, but it also creates a loving iteration of Mambéty's film, from a diasporic perspective.

Beyond these familial reflections, *Touki Bouki*'s aesthetic inheritance can be traced across Black visual cultures, from African auteurs to the surreal imaginaries of Afrofuturism to pop appropriation. Critics have found Mambéty's influence in the work of major West African film-makers like Momar Thiam, Souleymane Cissé and Abderrahmane Sissako, whom Catherine Ruelle considers to be 'totally inspired' by him.[183] Sissako's *Bamako* (2006) and *Timbuktu* (2014), for example, build on Mambéty's mix of realism and fantastical allegory for the twenty-first century. Another combination of folklore and political critique can be found in the films of Cameroonian director Jean-Pierre Bekolo, from the satirical *Quartier Mozart* in 1992 to 2016's dystopian *Naked Reality*. Bekolo interviews Mambéty in the short documentary *La Grammaire de grand mère* (1996), an echo of Mambéty's own *Parlons grand-mère*. The latter is about the filming of Idrissa Ouédraogo's *Yaaba* (1989), but also explores the tension between the knowledge systems represented by 'grammar' and 'grandma'.

Touki Bouki's influence is visible on films about immigration like Alain Gomis's *L'Afrance/As a Man* (2001), which animates the competing challenges for young Africans of life at home or in Europe, and Moussa Touré's *La Pirogue* (2012), which departs from Dakar and dramatises the anguish of the ocean journey in the titular small boat. In Black diasporic film-making, we can see echoes of Anta in the women's gazes in Julie Dash's African American masterpiece *Daughters of the Dust* (1991). British film-maker John Akomfrah drew on the character of Mory for the trickster figure of the Data Thief in his film *The Last Angel of History* (1996), and Akomfrah describes *Touki Bouki* as 'the one indisputable masterpiece of the African avant-garde'.[184] References can be found in popular genres too. Beyoncé has often drawn from histories of African and Afro-diasporic image-making, most famously in her references to *Daughters of the Dust* and to West African adornment in *Lemonade* (2016). She and Jay-Z updated the iconic image of Anta and Mory on the motorbike with zebu horns in the artwork for their On the Run II tour. (Mati Diop was not a fan of this appropriation, complaining that 'it looks like it's an art director who brought them the image, and no one has been concerned about what artistic and political story is behind it'.[185]) *Touki Bouki*'s artistic and political legacy has remained at the forefront for African artists: an installation by Djibril Dramé and slam poet Minus at the Dakar Biennale in 2018 restaged scenes from *Badou Boy* and *Touki Bouki*, and queer Nigerian film-maker Olive Nwosu cites the importance of *Touki Bouki* for her film *Egúngún/Masquerade* (2021).[186]

These resonances support the idea that *Touki Bouki* was a film in advance of its time: both its style and its themes look relevant and fresh today. Mambéty's film does more than align with contemporary tastes, though; in its radical vision of what cinematic language might do, it continues to challenge us. Mambéty's film-making remains open to discovery and reinterpretation by new generations, and *Touki Bouki*'s journey of beauty and liberation continues to speak across the many centres of world cinema.

Notes

1 Mass Ly, 'Le Cinéma africain a vivifié notre façon de voir le monde: entretien avec Catherine Ruelle', *Africiné*, 10 August 2008.
2 Anonymous, 'Festival de cinéma de Tanger: *Touki Bouki* de Djibril Diop Mambéty, meilleur film africain de l'histoire', *Agence de Presse Africaine*, 2 May 2018.
3 Nwachukwu Frank Ukadike, *Questioning African Cinema: Conversations with Film-makers* (Minneapolis: University of Minnesota Press, 2002), p. 122; Manthia Diawara, 'The Iconography of West African Cinema', in June Givanni (ed.), *Symbolic Narratives/African Cinema: Audiences, Theory and the Moving Image* (London: BFI, 2000), p. 85.
4 David Murphy and Patrick Williams, *Postcolonial African Cinema: Ten Directors* (Manchester: Manchester University Press, 2019), p. 91; Chérifa Benabdessadok, '*Touki Bouki* offert aux enfants d'Afrique', *Afrique-Asie*, 6 April 1987, p. 57.
5 El Hadji Massiga Faye, 'Témoinages sur l'homme et son oeuvre', *Africiné*, 12 August 2008.
6 Kenneth W. Harrow, 'The Queer Thing about Djibril Diop Mambéty: A Counterhegemonic Discourse Meets the Heterosexual Economy', *Paragraph* 24, no. 3 (2001), p. 76.
7 Mansour Sora Wade quoted in El Hadji Massiga Faye, 'Faire de Dakar la capitale du cinéma des pays du Sud', *Africiné*, 12 August 2008.
8 David Murphy, 'Africans Filming Africa: Questioning Theories of an Authentic African Cinema', *Journal of African Cultural Studies* 13, no. 2 (2000), p. 243.
9 Férid Boughedir, 'Le Cinéma africain a quinze ans', *Filméchange* 4 (1978), p. 77.
10 Vlad Dima, *Sonic Space in Djibril Diop Mambéty's Films* (Indianapolis: Indiana University Press, 2017), p. 2.
11 Louis Skorecki, '*Touki Bouki*', *Libération*, 19 March 1986, p. 32.
12 Sada Niang, *Nationalist African Cinema: Legacy and Transformations* (Lanham, MD: Lexington Books, 2014), p. 82.
13 Mark Cousins, 'Discovering Africa's Orson Welles', *Screen* 48, no. 4 (2007), p. 508.
14 Nwachukwu Frank Ukadike, 'Djibril and the Esthetic: *Touki Bouki*, a Film of Break', *Écrans d'Afrique* 24 (1998), p. 53.
15 J.-L. Pouillaude, '*Touki-Bouki*', *Positif*, June 1986, p. 79.
16 Kobena Mercer, *Welcome to the Jungle: New Positions in Black Cultural Studies* (London: Routledge, 1994), pp. 54–5.
17 For example, Vincent Canby, 'A Dream of Escape to Paris', *New York Times*, 15 February 1991, p. C10; Gene Moskowitz, '*Touki Bouki*', *Variety*, 23 May 1973, p. 34.
18 Cousins, 'Discovering Africa's Orson Welles', p. 508.
19 Ngũgĩ wa Thiong'o, *Moving the Centre: The Struggle for Cultural Freedoms* (London: James Currey, 1993).
20 Ella Shohat and Robert Stam, 'Narrativizing Visual Culture: Towards a Polycentric Aesthetics', in Nicholas Mirzoeff (ed.), *The Visual Culture Reader* (New York: Routledge, 1998), pp. 37–59.
21 Achille Mbembe and Sarah Nuttall, 'Introduction: Afropolis', in Sarah Nuttall and Achille Mbembe (eds), *Johannesburg: The Elusive Metropolis*

(Durham, NC: Duke University Press, 2008), p. 1.
22 Anonymous, 'Le Cyclope a vue *Touki Bouki*', *Le Soleil*, 24 April 1975, p. 8.
23 Djibril Diop Mambéty in Ukadike, *Questioning African Cinema*, p. 124.
24 Falila Gbadamassi, 'Teemour Diop Mambéty: "Etre décomplexé, s'ouvrir au monde: c'est ce qu'il faut retenir de mon père"', *Africiné*, 15 May 2018.
25 Ly, 'Le Cinéma africain'.
26 June Givanni, 'African Conversations: Djibril Diop Mambéty on White Sheets, Cinema and *Touki-Bouki*', *Sight and Sound* 5, no. 9 (1995), p. 30.
27 *Ninki Nanka: The Prince of Colobane* (Laurence Gavron, 1991).
28 Murphy and Williams, *Postcolonial African Cinema*, p. 91.
29 Alassane Seck Guèye, 'La Cinéaste et écrivain, Laurence Gavron, raconte Djibril Diop Mambéty et son oeuvre cinématographique', *Africiné*, 30 July 2008.
30 Gavron quoted in ibid.
31 Françoise Pfaff, *Twenty-five Black African Filmmakers* (New York: Greenwood Press, 1988), p. 217.
32 Xavier Villetard, 'Djibril Diop Mambéty n'a pas vieilli', *Libération*, 19 March 1986, p. 32.
33 Claire Andrade-Watkins, 'Francophone African Cinema: French Financial and Technical Assistance, 1961 to 1977', Ph.D. thesis, Boston University (1989), p. 223.
34 Murphy and Williams, *Postcolonial African Cinema*, p. 92.
35 Sada Niang, *Djibril Diop Mambéty: un cinéaste à contre-courant* (Paris: L'Harmattan, 2002), p. 213.

36 Ben Diogaye Bèye quoted in ibid.
37 Cheikh Ngaïdo Bâ quoted in Faye, 'Faire de Dakar'.
38 Paulin Soumanou Vieyra, *Le Cinéma africain: des origines à 1973* (Paris: Présence Africaine, 1975), p. 182.
39 Claire Andrade-Watkins, 'France's Bureau of Cinema: Financial and Technical Assistance 1961–77 – Operations and Implications for African Cinema', in Imruh Bakari and Mbye Cham (eds), *African Experiences of Cinema* (London: BFI, 1996), p. 112.
40 Ibid., pp. 112–13.
41 Andrade-Watkins, 'Francophone African Cinema', p. 201.
42 Vieyra, *Le Cinéma africain*, p. 182.
43 Balufu Bakupa-Kanyinda, 'Djibril Diop Mambéty: tribut cinématographique à Colobane', *Présence Africaine* 158 (1998), pp. 173–7. See also Giuseppe Gariazzo, '*Touki Bouki*', *Enciclopedia del cinema* (Rome: Treccani, 2004).
44 Villetard, 'Djibril Diop Mambéty n'a pas vieilli', p. 32.
45 Advertisements in *Le Soleil*, 22 March 1975, p. 6, and 29 March 1975, p. 4.
46 Ibid., 3 April 1975, p. 2.
47 Ibid., 12 April 1975, p. 4, and 19 April 1975, p. 4.
48 Ibid., 17 May 1975, p. 5.
49 Ben Diogaye Bèye quoted in Niang, *Djibril Diop Mambéty*, p. 217; Pouillaude, '*Touki-Bouki*', p. 79.
50 Latyr Mbassou Diouf, 'À le recherche du souffle libérateur', *Le Soleil*, 14 April 1975, p. 2.
51 M. Dia, 'Un Prix pour *Touki Bouky?*', *Le Soleil*, 22 April 1975, p. 2; Jean Bernard, 'Un Film africain: *Touki Bouki*', *Nouvelle Afrique*, 23–9 April 1975, p. 24.

52 Dia, 'Un Prix', p. 2; A. P. Diop, 'Je n'ai rien compris', *Le Soleil*, 29 April 1975, p. 2.
53 Kemal Ndiaye, 'Comme un roman de Marcel Proust', *Le Soleil*, 29 April 1975, p. 2; Pierre Souillac, 'De la nécessaire éducation du public', *Le Soleil*, 17 May 1975, p. 5; Anonymous, 'Le Cyclope a vue *Touki Bouki*', p. 8.
54 Ndiaye, 'Comme un roman de Marcel Proust', p. 2, and Souillac, 'De la nécessaire éducation du public', p. 5.
55 Anne Marty, '*Touki Bouki* ou la libération de l'imaginaire', *Le Soleil*, 25 April 1975, p. 2; Wolfgang von Wangenheim, 'Pas prophète en leur pays', *Le Soleil*, 15 May 1975, p. 2.
56 Anonymous, 'Le Cyclope a vue *Touki Bouki*', p. 8.
57 Pape Samba Ba, 'Un Champ non encore labouré', *Le Soleil*, 24 April 1975, p. 2; Charles Carrère, 'Nous sommes tous des délinquants', *Le Soleil*, 19 April 1975, p. 2; M. Raymond Diop, 'Une Contribution au développement', *Le Soleil*, 24 April 1975, p. 2.
58 Cheikh Kane, 'Dépasser la phase embryonnaire', *Le Soleil*, 9 April 1975, p. 3; Moustafa Diouf, 'Les Meilleurs du continent', *Le Soleil*, 22 April 1975, p. 2.
59 James Williams, *Ethics and Aesthetics in Contemporary African Cinema: The Politics of Beauty* (London: Bloomsbury, 2019), p. 129.
60 Louis Marcorelles, '*Touki Bouki* de Djibril Diop Mambéty', *Le Monde*, 25 March 1986, p. 18; Skorecki, '*Touki Bouki*', p. 32.
61 Moskowitz, '*Touki Bouki*', p. 34; Benabdessadok, '*Touki Bouki* offert aux enfants d'Afrique', p. 57.
62 Faye, 'Témoinages sur l'homme et son oeuvre'.
63 Gbadamassi, 'Teemour Diop Mambéty'.
64 Djibril Diop Mambéty in Beti Ellerson, 'Remembering Djibril Diop Mambéty on the 20th Anniversary of His Death', *Black Camera* 9, no. 2 (2018), p. 480.
65 Ibid., p. 479.
66 Souleymane Cissé quoted on Il Cinema Ritrovato website. Available at: <https://festival.ilcinemaritrovato.it/en/film/touki-bouki/> (accessed 20 September 2024).
67 Murphy and Williams, *Postcolonial African Cinema*, p. 97.
68 Matthew Mananga, 'The Rural vs the Urban: The Postcolonial City of Dakar in the Film *Touki Bouki*', *ArchDaily*, 27 January 2023.
69 Mbembe and Nuttall, 'Introduction: Afropolis', p. 1.
70 Williams, *Ethics and Aesthetics in Contemporary African Cinema*, p. 93.
71 For further discussion of the film's representation of Dakar, see Anna Livia, 'Everyone Would Rather Be in Paris', *Visual Anthropology* 16, no. 4 (2003), pp. 393–406.
72 Emmanuelle Chérel, 'L'Énergie radicale de *Touki Bouki*', *Multitudes* 1, no. 58 (2015), p. 34.
73 André Gardies, *Cinéma d'Afrique noir francophone: l'espace-miroir* (Paris: L'Harmattan, 1989), p. 128.
74 Malini Guha, 'Narratives of Return in the Films of Ousmane Sembene and Djibril Diop Mambéty', in Rebecca Prime (ed.), *Cinematic Homecomings: Exile and Return in*

Transnational Cinema (London: Bloomsbury, 2015), p. 230.
75 Djibril Diop Mambéty quoted in Giuseppe Gariazzo, *Poetiche del cinema africano* (Turin: Lindau, 1998), p. 44, and *Ninki Nanka: The Prince of Colobane*.
76 Niang, *Djibril Diop Mambéty*, p. 99.
77 Kate M. Bonin, 'Dreams of Dakar, 1973: Reading Donato Ndongo-Bidyogo's "El sueño" with Djibril Diop Mambéty's *Touki Bouki*', *Research in African Literatures* 49, no. 2 (2018), p. 60.
78 Sílvio Marcus de Souza Correa, 'Senegalese Wrestling as "National Sport" and Other Modern Myths in *Lamb*', *Black Camera* 13, no. 2 (2022), pp. 396–416.
79 For discussion of the film's use of Wolof and French as neocolonial class markers, see Lindiwe Dovey, 'Subjects of Exile: Alienation in Francophone West African Cinema', *International Journal of Francophone Studies* 12, no. 1 (2009), pp. 55–75.
80 Livia, 'Everyone Would Rather Be in Paris', p. 404.
81 Mahriana Rofheart, *Shifting Perceptions of Migration in Senegalese Literature, Film, and Social Media* (London: Lexington Books/Fortress Academic, 2013), p. 21.
82 Louis Skorecki, 'L'Histoire rouge et noir de *Touki Bouki*', *Libération*, 19 March 1986, p. 32; Marcorelles, '*Touki Bouki* de Djibril Diop Mambéty', p. 18.
83 Moskowitz, '*Touki Bouki*', p. 34.
84 Guha, 'Narratives of Return', p. 238.
85 Livia, 'Everyone Would Rather Be in Paris', p. 403.
86 Walter Benjamin, *The Arcades Project*, trans. Kevin McLaughlin and Howard Eiland (Cambridge, MA: Belknap Press of Harvard University Press, 1999), pp. 462–3.
87 See Gardies, *Cinéma d'Afrique noir francophone*, p. 44, and Williams, *Ethics and Aesthetics in Contemporary African Cinema*, pp. 94–9.
88 Niang, *Djibril Diop Mambéty*, p. 109.
89 Djibril Diop Mambéty in Ukadike, *Questioning African Cinema*, p. 131.
90 Anonymous, 'Pour un cinéma africain qui parle le langage du peuple', *Le Soleil*, 3 April 1975, p. 10.
91 Djibril Diop Mambéty quoted in Pfaff, *Twenty-five Black African Filmmakers*, p. 126.
92 Djibril Diop Mambéty quoted in Alessandra Speciale, 'Djibril, the Prince and the Poet of African Cinema', *Écrans d'Afrique* 24 (1998), p. 52.
93 Aimé Césaire quoted in Mbwil Ngal, *Aimé Césaire: un homme à la recherche d'une patrie* (Paris: Les Nouvelles éditions africaines, 1975), p. 42; Léopold Sédar Senghor quoted in Janet G. Vaillant, *Black, French, and African: A Life of Léopold Sédar Senghor* (Cambridge, MA: Harvard University Press, 1990), p. 110.
94 Ezekiel Mphahlele, 'The Fabric of African Culture', *Foreign Affairs*, July 1964, p. 624; Stanislas Spero Adotevi quoted in Elizabeth Harney, *In Senghor's Shadow: Art, Politics, and the Avant-Garde in Senegal, 1960–1995* (Durham, NC: Duke University Press, 2004), p. 76, n. 88.
95 Cheikh Anta Diop, *The Cultural Unity of Black Africa* (London: Karnak House, 1989).
96 Amílcar Cabral, *Return to the Source: Selected Speeches* (New York: Monthly Review Press, 1973), pp. 57–69.

97 Manthia Diawara, *African Cinema: Politics and Culture* (Bloomington: Indiana University Press, 1992), pp. 159–65.
98 Keyan G. Tomaselli, '"African" Cinema: Theoretical Perspectives on Some Unresolved Questions', in Imruh Bakari and Mbye Cham (eds), *African Experiences of Cinema* (London: BFI, 1996), p. 168; Frantz Fanon, *Wretched of the Earth* (Paris: Présence Africaine, 1963), p. 189.
99 Souleymane Bachir Diagne, 'Rereading Aimé Césaire: Negritude as Creolization', *small axe* 48 (November 2015), pp. 121–3; Cheikh Thiam, 'Negritude Africentered: Revisiting Senghor and Glissant's Countercultures of Modernity in the 21st Century', *Présence Africaine* 198 (2018), p. 53. For further discussion of Négritude, see Messay Kebede, 'Re-imagining the Philosophy of Decolonization', in Adeshina Afolayan and Toyin Falola (eds), *The Palgrave Handbook of African Philosophy* (New York: Palgrave Macmillan, 2017), pp. 447–59.
100 Reiland Rabaka, *The Negritude Movement: W.E.B. Du Bois, Leon Damas, Aime Cesaire, Leopold Senghor, Frantz Fanon, and the Evolution of an Insurgent Idea* (London: Lexington Books, 2015). See also Gary Wilder, *Freedom Time: Negritude, Decolonization, and the Future of the World* (Durham, NC: Duke University Press, 2015).
101 Diagne, 'Rereading Aimé Césaire', p. 126.
102 Givanni, 'African Conversations', p. 31.
103 The discussion of Agit'Art draws from Harney, *In Senghor's Shadow*, pp. 105–14.
104 Ima Ebong, 'Negritude between Mask and Flag, Senegalese Cultural Ideology and the "École de Dakar"', in Susan Vogel (ed.), *Africa Explores: 20th Century African Art* (New York: Center for African Art, 1991), pp. 198–209.
105 Murphy, 'Africans Filming Africa', pp. 23–40.
106 Diawara, 'Iconography of West African Cinema', p. 81.
107 Manthia Diawara, 'Popular Culture and Oral Traditions in African Film', in Imruh Bakari and Mbye Cham (eds), *African Experiences of Cinema* (London: BFI, 1996), p. 210.
108 Amadou Hampâté Bâ, 'The Living Tradition', in J. Ki-Zerbo (ed.), *General History of Africa/UNESCO International Scientific Committee for the Drafting of a General History of Africa*, vol. 1, *Methodology and African Prehistory* (London: Heinemann, 1981), p. 166.
109 Melissa Thackway, *Africa Shoots Back: Alternative Perspectives in Sub-Saharan Francophone African Film* (Bloomington: Indiana University Press, 2003), p. 54; Thiam, 'Negritude Africentered', p. 58, discusses the ethnocentrism of writing-centred cultures that Derrida diagnoses in *Of Grammatology* (Baltimore, MD: Johns Hopkins University Press, 1974).
110 Bâ, 'Living Tradition', p. 185, notes that the word *griot* is actually French and prefers the Bambara word *dieli*. In reference to cinema, however, *griot* has become the most popular term.
111 Ousmane Sembene, 'Film-makers and African Culture', *Africa* 71 (1977), p. 80.

112 Both Thackway, *Africa Shoots Back*, p. 57, and Olivier Barlet, *African Cinemas: Decolonizing the Gaze* (London: Zed Books, 2000), pp. 162–5, describe the *griot* in these terms.
113 Mambéty quoted in Givanni, 'African Conversations', p. 31.
114 Murphy and Williams, *Postcolonial African Cinema*, p. 9.
115 See Diawara, 'Popular Culture and Oral Traditions in African Film', p. 215, and Thackway, *Africa Shoots Back*, pp. 84–7.
116 Denise Paulme, *La Mère devorante: essai sur la morphologie des contes africains* (Paris: Éditions Gallimard, 1976), p. 25, quoted in Thackway, *Africa Shoots Back*, p. 77.
117 Chérel, 'L'Énergie radicale de *Touki Bouki*', p. 38.
118 Thackway, *Africa Shoots Back*, p. 68.
119 Rolf Luapa, '*Touki Bouki*, treize ans après', *Afrique-Asie*, 19 May 1986, p. 78.
120 Dima, *Sonic Space in Djibril Diop Mambéty's Films*, p. 38.
121 Williams, *Ethics and Aesthetics in Contemporary African Cinema*, pp. 149–50.
122 Mambéty quoted in Ukadike, *Questioning African Cinema*, p. 129.
123 Bâ, 'Living Tradition', p. 168.
124 Wasis Diop quoted in Fatou Kiné Sène, 'Wasis Diop: "Ce que je dois à Djibril …"', *Africiné*, 30 August 2008.
125 Dima, *Sonic Space in Djibril Diop Mambéty's Films*, p. 7.
126 Mbye B. Cham, 'Djibril Diop Mambéty: Sounds in the Keys of Ordinary Folk', *Nka: Journal of Contemporary African Art* 21 (2007), p. 69.
127 Babacar M'Baye, 'Charting Aminata Fall's Cosmopolitanism: A Comparative Study of African American and Senegambian Blues Lyrics', *The Global South* 14, no 1 (2020), pp. 39–67.
128 Valérie Nivelon, 'Saint-Louis du Sénégal, La Nouvelle Orléans: deux villes en miroir', *Radio France International*, 23 June 2012. Available at: <www.rfi.fr/emission/20120623-2-saint-louis-senegal-nouvelle-orleans-deux-villes-miroir> (accessed 11 August 2024).
129 Thackway, *Africa Shoots Back*, p. 81.
130 Skorecki, 'L'Histoire rouge et noir de *Touki Bouki*', p. 32.
131 Alexander Fisher, 'Reclaiming Josephine Baker in the Filmic Ethnomusicology of Djibril Diop Mambéty', *Music and the Moving Image* 12, no. 2 (2019), p. 11.
132 Ibid., p. 18.
133 André Levison quoted in Jon Kear, 'Venus noire: Josephine Baker and the Parisian Music Hall', in Michael Sheringham (ed.), *Parisian Fields* (London: Reaktion, 1996), p. 54; Kathryn Kalinak, 'Disciplining Josephine Baker: Gender, Race and the Limits of Disciplinarity', in James Buhler, Caryl Flinn and David Neumayer (eds), *Music and Cinema* (Middletown, CT: Wesleyan University Press, 2000), p. 323.
134 Karen C. C. Dalton and Henry Louis Gates Jr, 'Josephine Baker and Paul Colin: Dance Seen Through Parisian Eyes', *Critical Inquiry* 24, no. 4 (1998), p. 933.
135 Elizabeth Coffman, 'Uncanny Performances in Colonial Narratives: Josephine Baker in *Princess Tam Tam*', *Paradoxa: Studies in World Literary Genres* 3, nos. 3–4 (1997), p. 379.

136 Kalinak, 'Disciplining Josephine Baker', p. 316.
137 Anne Anlin Cheng, *Second Skin: Josephine Baker and the Modern Surface* (Oxford: Oxford University Press, 2011), p. 3.
138 Elizabeth Ezra, *The Colonial Unconscious: Race and Culture in Interwar France* (London: Cornell University Press, 2000), p. 99.
139 Anny Wynchank, 'Touki-Bouki: The New Wave on the Cinematic Shores of Africa', *South African Theatre Journal* 12, nos. 1–2 (1998), pp. 53–72.
140 Ibid., p. 54.
141 Wes Felton, 'Caught in the Undertow: African Francophone Cinema in the French New Wave', *Senses of Cinema* 57 (2010), n.p.
142 Souillac, 'De la nécessaire éducation du public', p. 5.
143 Heather Snell, 'Toward "a Giving and a Receiving": Teaching Djibril Diop Mambéty's *Touki Bouki*', *Journal of African Cultural Studies* 26, no. 2 (2014), p. 132.
144 Saïdou Alceny Barry, 'Djibril Diop Mambéty: un autre cinéma', *Africiné*, 22 August 2009.
145 Raoul Granqvist, *Photography and American Coloniality: Eliot Elisofon in Africa, 1942–1972* (East Lansing: Michigan State University Press, 2017), p. 192; Ndiaye, 'Comme un roman de Marcel Proust', p. 2.
146 Thackway, *Africa Shoots Back*, p. 23.
147 Patrick Williams, 'Entering and Leaving Modernity: Utopia and Dystopia in Mambéty's *Touki Bouki* and *Hyènes*', in Wendy Everett (ed.), *The Seeing Century: Film, Vision and Identity* (Amsterdam: Rodopi, 2000), p. 126; Chinweizu, Onwuchekwa Jemie and Ihechukwu Madubuike, *Toward the Decolonization of African Literature* (Washington, DC: Howard University Press, 1983).
148 Rachel Gabara, *Documentary Objectives: Filming Africa from Colonialism to Independence* (Indianapolis: Indiana University Press, 2025), p. 5.
149 Chérel, 'L'Énergie radicale de *Touki Bouki*', p. 33.
150 James E. Genova, *Cinema and Development in West Africa* (Bloomington: Indiana University Press, 2013), p. 129.
151 Gariazzo, *Poetiche del cinema africano*, p. 45.
152 Niang, *Djibril Diop Mambéty*, pp. 112–13.
153 Zakiyyah Iman Jackson, *Becoming Human: Matter and Meaning in an Antiblack World* (New York: New York University Press, 2020); Rizvana Bradley, *Anteaesthetics: Black Aesthesis and the Critique of Form* (Palo Alto, CA: Stanford University Press, 2023).
154 See Martin P. Botha, 'Queering African Film Aesthetics: A Survey from the 1950s to 2003', in Nwachukwu Frank Ukadike (ed.), *Critical Approaches to African Cinema Discourse* (Lanham, MD: Lexington Books, 2014), pp. 63–86.
155 Françoise Pfaff, 'Eroticism and Sub-Saharan African Films', in Imruh Bakari and Mbye Cham (ed.), *African Experiences of Cinema* (London: BFI, 1996), p. 259.
156 Ibid., p. 257.
157 Harrow, 'Queer Thing about Djibril Diop Mambéty', p. 76; Greg Thomas, 'Hyenas in the Enchanted Brothel: "The Naked Truth" in Djibril Diop Mambéty', *Black Camera* 2, no. 2 (2011), p. 14.

158 Dima, *Sonic Space in Djibril Diop Mambéty's Films*, p. 26.
159 Murphy and Williams, *Postcolonial African Cinema*, p. 101.
160 See Karl Schoonover and Rosalind Galt, *Queer Cinema in the World* (Durham, NC: Duke University Press, 2016), pp. 164–71, 216.
161 Lindsey Green-Simms, *Queer African Cinemas* (Durham, NC: Duke University Press, 2022), p. 7.
162 Chérel, 'L'Énergie radicale de *Touki Bouki*', p. 34; André Rollin, '*Touki-Bouki*', *Le Canard enchaîné*, 19 March 1986, p. 7.
163 Livia, 'Everyone Would Rather Be in Paris', p. 400.
164 Karl Schoonover, 'Wastrels of Time: Slow Cinema's Laboring Body, the Political Spectator, and the Queer', *Framework* 53, no. 1 (2012), p. 73.
165 Williams, *Ethics and Aesthetics in Contemporary African Cinema*, p. 204.
166 Rosalind Galt, *Pretty: Film and the Decorative Image* (New York: Columbia University Press, 2011).
167 Harrow, 'Queer Thing about Djibril Diop Mambéty', p. 77.
168 Williams, *Ethics and Aesthetics in Contemporary African Cinema*, p. 303, n. 29; Thomas, 'Hyenas in the Enchanted Brothel', p. 13.
169 Niang, *Djibril Diop Mambéty*, p. 121.
170 Birago Diop, *Contes d'Amadou Koumba* (Paris: Présence Africaine, 1969).
171 J. D. Sapir, 'Leper, Hyena, and Blacksmith in Kujamaat Diola Thought', *American Ethnologist* 8 (1981), pp. 532–3.
172 Jürgen W. Frembgen, 'The Magicality of Hyenas: Beliefs and Practices in West and South Asia', *Asian Folklore Studies* 57 (1998), p. 333.
173 Stephen E. Glickman, 'The Spotted Hyena from Aristotle to *The Lion King*: Reputation is Everything', *Social Research* 62, no. 3 (1995), p. 508.
174 Ibid., p. 505.
175 Olivier Barlet, '*Touki Bouki*: de quelle hyène parle-t-on', *Africultures*, 27 July 2008; Thomas, 'Hyenas in the Enchanted Brothel', p. 21.
176 Mambéty in Ellerson, 'Remembering Djibril Diop Mambéty', pp. 478–9.
177 Niang, *Djibril Diop Mambéty*, p. 129.
178 Djibril Diop Mambéty in Ukadike, *Questioning African Cinema*, pp. 124–5.
179 Harrow, 'Queer Thing about Djibril Diop Mambéty', p. 78.
180 Sandra M. Grayson, 'Djibril Diop Mambéty: A Retrospective', *Research in African Literatures* 32, no. 4 (2001), p. 138.
181 Mansour Diouf in *Ninki Nanka: The Prince of Colobane*.
182 James Williams, 'A Thousand Suns: Traversing the Archive and Transforming Documentary in Mati Diop's *Mille soleils*', *Film Quarterly* 7, no. 1 (2016), p. 89.
183 Ly, 'Le Cinéma africain'. See also Niang, *Nationalist African Cinema*, p. 82.
184 Ashley Clark, '*Touki Bouki*: Word, Sound and Power', The Criterion Collection, 9 March 2021. Available at: <https://www.criterion.com/current/posts/7309-touki-bouki-word-sound-and-power> (accessed 15 September 2024).
185 Ryan Gilbey, 'How Beyoncé and Jay-Z Put a Visionary African Film Back in the Spotlight', *Guardian*, 17 June 2018.
186 Laura Fortes, 'Olive Nwosu parle d'*Egúngún* avec une histoire d'amour

impossible: entretien avec la réalisatrice nigériane', *Africiné*, 28 July 2023; Greg Thomas, 'Djibril Diop Mambéty's Cinema of Possibility', *Harvard Film Archive*, September 2019. Available at: <https://harvardfilmarchive.org/programs/djibril-diop-mambety> (accessed 24 September 2024).

Image credits
Badou Boy (Djibril Diop Mambéty, 1970), Studio Kankourama; *Pierrot le fou* (Jean-Luc Godard, 1965), Productions Georges de Beauregard/Dino De Laurentiis Cinematografica; *Strike* (Sergei Eisenstein, 1925), Proletkult/First Studio Goskino; *Hyenas* (Djibril Diop Mambéty, 1992), © Thelma Film AG/ADR Productions/Maag Daan; *Xala* (Ousmane Sembene, 1975), Filmi Doomireew/Société National de Cinéma; *Le Franc* (Djibril Diop Mambéty, 1994), Waka Films/Scolopendra Productions/Maag Daan; *Black Girl* (Ousmane Sembene, 1966), Filmi Doomireew/Les Actualités Françaises; *Zouzou* (Marc Allégret, 1934), Productions Arys; *A Thousand Suns* (Mati Diop, 2013), Anna Sanders Films.

Credits

Touki Bouki
Senegal
1973

Written, Directed and Produced by
Djibril Diop Mambéty
Cinematography
Pap Samba Sow
Sound Recording
El Hadj M'Bow
Assistants
Mawa Gaye
Abdoulaye Sy
Grip
Alioune N'Diaye
Production Managers
Lamine Ba Carlos
Ousmane Sow
Set Design/Costumes/ Stills Photography
Aziz Diop Mambéty
External Collaborators
Fenouil
Manuel de Kset
Assistant Directors
Momar Thiam
Ben Diogaye Bèye
Production Assistant
Medoune Faye
Production Company
Cinegrit

uncredited
Director of Photography
Georges Bracher
Editors
Siro Asteni
Emma Mennenti

CAST
Magaye Niang
Mory
**Myriam Niang
(as Mareme Niang)**
Anta
**Christoph Colomb
(as Christophe Colomb)**
**Mustapha Ture
(as Moustapha Toure)**
Aminata Fall
Aunt Oumy
Ousseynou Diop
Charlie
Fernand Dalfin
Al Demba
Dieynaba Dieng
Assane Faye
Robbie Lawson
Magoné N'Diaye
Aliou N'Diaye
Apsa Niang
Omar Seck
Colette Simon
Langouste

With the Voices of
Josephine Baker
(as Joséphine Baker)
Mado Robin
Aminata Fall

Production Details
35mm
1.37:1
Colour
Mono
Running time:
88 minutes

Release Details
Senegal release on
29 March 1975 by
Société d'Importation,
Distribution,
et Exploitation
Cinématographique
(SIDEC)